Who's Afraid of 1984?

Other books by the author

HERE COMES IMMORTALITY

IT USUALLY BEGINS WITH AYN RAND

RADICAL LIBERTARIANISM

Contributor to

THE CON III CONTROVERSY: The Critics Look at the Greening of America

READINGS IN AMERICAN IDEOLOGIES

Editor (with Murray Rothbard)

THE RIGHT WING INDIVIDUALIST TRADITION IN AMERICA

Who's Afraid of 1984?

JEROME TUCCILLE

ARLINGTON HOUSE · PUBLISHERS
NEW ROCHELLE, NEW YORK

Manufactured in the United States of America

Library of Congress Cataloging in Publication Data

Tuccille, Jerome.
Who's afraid of 1984?

Bibliography: p.
1. Civilization, Modern--1950- I. Title.
CB161.T8 909.82'8 75-5724
ISBN 0-87000-308-9

Contents

Who's Afraid of 1984?

BOOK ONE
Doomsday Past

1

The Doomsday Brigade

1

1984.

Even those who have not read George Orwell's famous novel, or seen the movie, know what this year signifies. Images of Big Brother, a universal slave state, government television cameras in our homes observing us as we eat, sleep, and perform a mandatory calisthenics regimen, flash immediately through our minds. 1984. Never before in history has a single year held such ominous connotations for such a broad cross-section of humanity. A book, a movie, a scenario of the future set down in chilling detail by a singular British author is marked indelibly in the public consciousness. The imagination is stirred. We are fascinated and repelled simultaneously. The man has hypnotized us with a view of hell on earth and made us focus our sights on a single year, one year out of the tens of thousands humanity has already passed through. The man is dead now but his chilling vision lives on. We dote upon his word. His landmark year approaches, drawing a little nearer every day. The wheel of time spins quickly, too quickly for most of us, eating away at the future, transforming it into the present and past. Soon 1984 will be here and George Orwell will be proved either right or wrong; he will go down in history either as a stunning prophet or a gifted writer who turned out to be a poor political forecaster. The optimists—a small but hardy minority among us to be sure—say George Orwell will be wrong. I am an optimist.

2

Crises, manufactured crises, reinforce the Orwellian vision. Pick up a newspaper or flick on the television set. Any network will do; it doesn't matter. You will be overwhelmed by crises every day. The earth is doomed. Humanity is destined to transmogrify itself into a race of swarming ants or cockroaches. Shades of Franz Kafka. Pick your own crisis; there are many to choose from and everyone has his favorite—famine, overpopulation, pollution, energy shortages, soaring medical costs, rebellions and civil uprisings. If I have left any out, please excuse me, as I have not yet read my morning paper.

Crises are not new. They have been with us since man first learned to communicate with his neighbors. But the Doomsday Brigade has been growing over the centuries; its cries are becoming more shrill, its message more hysterical and more widely disseminated because of an instantaneous communications technology—a technology the Doomsayers condemn even as they utilize it to peddle their Orwellian warnings. In the early 1960s there was an outcry against automation. By creating machines to do the work of man, you see, we were going to have massive unemployment by the late 1960s. Thirty percent of the

American workforce would be turned into the streets, destined to wander eternally without direction or purpose, a vast army of the disenfranchised crowding the barrooms of the nation, begging for dimes on streetcorners, and swelling the welfare rolls. This doomsday projection never came to pass, of course, since automation evolved into a whole new computerization industry which created an estimated 40 percent more jobs than those it replaced.

Did this beneficent development defuse the doomsday movement; retard it slightly, and give pause to its leading prophets; send them back to their drawing boards, perhaps, and cause them to reevaluate their projections in view of new information they had not considered before? No; it made them angrier. As the rest of the world has learned since then, there is no fury on earth to equal that of a visionary whose crystal ball turns out to have been slightly cracked. Paul Ehrlich returned with a vengeance, along with the Paddock brothers and a host of others whom we shall be examining more closely in later sections, predicting large-scale famines by the early 1970s, overpopulation catastrophes a few years later, social cataclysm due to pollution and various shortages by the 1980s, and eventual collapse for all of civilized society by . . . well, they change the date every year. The end of the world has been set for 1975, 1980, 1984, 1990, and 2000 by different stalwarts of the Doomsday Brigade, depending on their comparative levels of optimism. Only an *extreme* optimist in this camp thinks we can hold off the Black Death until the beginning of the next century. The more *realistic* of the group see imminent annihilation within the next eighteen months. The next eighteen months starting *when*? you ask. Why, the next eighteen months from whenever they happen to be issuing their pronouncements, of course.

"Does it ever bother you that your projections have all turned out to be wrong so far?" a newscaster asked Paul Ehrlich during a television interview.

"It doesn't matter," Ehrlich replied, totally unruffled. "That's not important. The only thing I'm concerned about is that civilization is heading for a collapse unless certain measures are taken, and taken now. Time is running out on all of us."

Certain measures? What kind of measures are Ehrlich and his colleagues talking about? We will look at them in detail in following sections, but in general terms one gets the impression that the doomsday prophets have read George Orwell's *1984*—and decided that it might not be such a bad world to live in if only they can be allowed to run the show.

3

The Doomsday Brigade can be regarded as the socio-ecological arm of the socialist state. Each new manufactured crisis generates a call for new reforms, new political solutions to social problems, more stringent controls over the lives of the citizenry. Michael Harrington, the author of *Socialism* and other books, has been calling for a "temporary benevolent dictatorship" since 1969 and his views are treated with the utmost seriousness by much of the American intelligentsia. His kind of dictatorship would be a "humane" one, of course, therefore not to be feared by "rightminded people" genuinely concerned about the welfare of their fellow man. A Harrington-style dictatorship would have the "public interest" at heart; its goals would be to provide economic equality and a decent standard of living for all, while simultaneously preserving the basic civil liberties spelled out in the Bill of Rights. Most liberals think Harrington may be "going a little too far" in his urgent call for a temporary dictatorship (your guess is as good as mine as to exactly *how* temporary it would turn out to be), but, nevertheless, they are willing to forgive him his excesses since his basic "decency" and his "ultimate goals" are beyond reproach. This is the same mentality which is willing to whitewash the "excesses" of Mao Tse-tung and his totalitarian regime because he, personally, is a "benevolent" man and his goals are good; the same type of reasoning which draws a basic distinction between a left-wing and a right-wing dictatorship—the former errs on the side of "excessive humanistic exuberance," the latter is invariably the apotheosis of unbridled moral depravity.

So, you see, it is possible for a Michael Harrington to escape a demand for benevolent dictatorship with little more than a slap on the wrist ("Cool it, Mike, you'll stir up a hornet's nest with that kind of rhetoric"), but let a *less* benevolent social critic like, say, John Chamberlain or Jeffrey St. John, dare to utter the same phrase and see what would happen. To be sure, the major architects of opinion in the country, including our newspaper editorialists and media commentators, would turn purple with a veritable apoplectic fit. First they would suffer a collective loss of consciousness due to a slackening of the blood supply to the critical brain centers while the message was being swallowed, analyzed, and regurgitated. Then, following a near-comatose state lasting all of seven-and-a-half minutes, the frothing-at-the-mouth, the gnashing-of-teeth, and sharpening-of-knives would begin. Roars of "Fascism!," "Neo-Nazism!," and "Hitlerite!" would resound across the land, over the seas, and against the heavens. Birds would be made to freeze in their flight and take note of this travesty of justice being perpetrated below. Benevolence, you see, like beauty and ugliness, is in the eye of the beholder.

4

Sadly enough, the socio-ecological arm of the socialist state has now gone international. Having failed (so far) to impose its absolute humanitarian rule on the nation, it has established a Doomsday Internationale, if you will, to socialize humanity on a global scale. It is no longer enough merely to control an individual country. Modern crises, unlike the crises of twenty and thirty years ago, are global crises requiring (you guessed it) global solutions. A higher sovereignty than the nation must be created, the argument goes, with final jurisdiction over the pressing problems of our time. This is not a recent position, actually; it is the old One World Government movement advanced to a new phase and dressed out with a brand-new rhetoric; the old label, which failed to evoke shouts of joyous enthusiasm from the multitudes, has been discarded in favor of the more benevolent-sounding handle: World Federalists.

You will note as we move along that advocates of One World Government or world federation, whatever jargon it goes by, never speak in terms of a *limited* world organization, a mere peacekeeping body guaranteeing individual liberties and economic freedom. No, the demand is invariably for a world social democracy, a global socialist or welfare state, modeled along the lines of the Swedish design only spread out to encompass every nook and cranny of the planet. The World Federalists are determined to close off all sanctuaries, all avenues of escape for reactionary individualists who prefer a private existence rather than that of an international social worker. Today the earth, tomorrow the solar system, next year the universe! may well be the battle cry of this brigade. It is well to be prepared.

The American wing of this movement, WFUSA, as it is known, is presided over by Dr. Luther Evans, a former director-general of UNESCO (the United Nations Educational, Scientific, and Cultural Organization), while publisher Norman Cousins is the president of the World Association of World Federalists. WFUSA publishes a monthly newspaper, and just to give you an idea of the general tone of the publication, the April 1974 issue carried a series of headlines like: HOW MANY PEOPLE WILL STARVE THIS YEAR?; A NEW ORDER FOR WORLD ECONOMY; THERE IS NO FOOD; WITHIN ONE YEAR, A BILLION PEOPLE CAN DIE FROM STARVATION; WILL AMERICA HELP SAVE THE WORLD?; MALTHUS RESURRECTED: FAMINE! There were many others of this sort, as there are in each issue, but you now have a general concept of the organization's basic *thrust*. It is the doomsday syndrome, discussed briefly at the beginning of this section, dressed out now in political garb.

5

Luther Evans. He is a kindly looking man, really; a short, stout, elderly, rumpled man with a craggy face beginning to sag with age, a tweedy man with wrinkled suits, a crushed fedora hat that must predate the Depression of 1929, a pipe-smoking gentleman eternally filling, tamping out, and refilling the bowl from an endless supply of tobacco in the side pocket of his jacket.

But his appearance is somewhat deceptive. When he speaks he starts off slowly, his voice deep and resonant like that of a younger man. He builds as he works along, his voice taking on volume and power, and soon he is haranguing his audience about the need for a single world body, with an evangelistic fervor more suitable for a revival meeting than a scholarly assemblage. He is fervent and dedicated to his cause. He has not spent his life in "service to humanity" for nothing.

"The world can no longer afford the luxury of separate countries around the globe," he says, "no more than each country can any longer afford the luxury of nineteenth-century individualism in its midst."

He builds on his theme: "Today's crises are global in scope, and they demand global planning for their solutions. We need a higher sovereignty than the nation, modeled along the lines of a humanitarian social democracy, which will have priority in all social and political matters. I'm talking about a World Federation of Nations. Each country on earth will have the same limited power as the American states do today, with final authority vested in the world body the same way that final authority in this country is vested in Washington, D.C."

By now it is perfectly apparent that Jeffersonian decentralization is anathema to Dr. Evans. He brings his ringing delivery to a finale: "If we are going to save ourselves from extinction, if we are going to create a decent, civilized world with plenty of food and abundance for everyone, then we have to get busy *now*. We need a higher sovereignty to take over the principal means of production and distribution on a global scale, a world planning body to guard against future crises, to narrow the gap between rich and poor. We can't wait much longer. It may already be too late. We've got to get going on this immediately."

Luther Evans finished. He tamped out his pipe and refilled it from the pouch in his pocket. Lighting it, he announced that he would be glad to answer questions. My hand was the first in the air.

"Do you see any danger of your world federation evolving into a dictatorship?"

"We need checks and balances, but it is a possibility. We have to take the risk. We can't afford not to."

"Don't you think the risk may be too high when you consider the consequences?"

"What's your solution?"

"Many of the crises we faced in the past were solved by private initiative. Many were rendered obsolete by the Industrial Revolution. Suppose, just suppose, we run *out of* crises during the next ten years. We might have created your world federation, gotten ourselves trapped into a worldwide dictatorship, and all for nothing. My solution is that private initiative is already solving some of the problems you talked about."

"Nonsense. Irresponsible nonsense," said Dr. Evans, puffing blue clouds of acrid smoke through his smog machine. As I said before, his kindly appearance was somewhat deceptive. We went around on this for several minutes, and then others in the audience added their own voices to the exchange. This was a meeting of the World Future Society, a nonideological organization dedicated to studying current trends in an effort to project future developments in all fields. Since it is open to all political persuasions, I had no idea of the ideological coloring of the gathering, but I quickly and happily discovered that, one by one as the participants voiced their own opinions, they ranged from neutral to general disagreement with the World Federalist position. This was a nonsectarian audience whose gut reaction, collectively speaking, was against a further centralization of power. I wondered whether this would have been the case back in the late 1960s when the campuses were swamped with neo-Marxist sloganeering. Refreshingly enough, it was a youthful audience as well—middle-thirties and under.

Dr. Evans was visibly disgruntled by the reception, and muttered to me as he left: "I had forgotten how many of today's young people are becoming enamored of capitalism."

6

Trends. Forecasts. Projections. Anyone who pretends to see with any degree of precision more than three or four years into the future, at our current rate of technological and social development, is either a fool or an outright fraud. Nevertheless, the public is interested in knowing the direction in which we are heading, and the field of socio-political forecasting has been fairly well dominated by the Doomsday Brigade—alarmists and pessimists who invariably are either socialist or welfare-statist in their political orientation. There are notable exceptions (Herman Kahn, F. M. Esfandiary, Colin Clark), but the balance is definitely on the side of the doomsayers. They have taken to the airways and other public forums over the years, and issued their final and conclusive pronouncements about the demise of civilization unless . . . unless we listen to them, of course. Their apocalyptic projections have not come to pass, yet they cannot be dismissed easily. They play on fear and uncertainty, the uncertainty we all necessarily have about exactly what is going to happen tomorrow and the day after. The Doomsday Brigade has had a near-monopoly on the public forum for far too long; it is time for a reevaluation of the human condition against the background of a long-range historical view. It is time to step outside of a tunnel-vision view of the future and try to broaden our scope, look out on the wider periphery of history and reevaluate the doomsday message we have all been bombarded with since the middle-1950s and beyond.

Without claiming any special prescience, any extrasensory powers or gifts of clairvoyance (no more than Paul Ehrlich possesses at least), it is my own view that the Doomsday Brigade is wrong. No one but a mental defective would deny that we are faced with pressing problems, but it is my contention that a great majority of them are (a) blown totally out of proportion, or (b) based on a misinterpretation of the facts as presented by the pessimists. I believe that this brand of nagging pessimism, as well as the entire concept of social democracy as a viable form of government, is dying out after a half-century of continuing failures. In this book I will take the position that, contrary to the doomsday projections, the human race is on the threshold of a social, cultural, and political rejuvenation, a New Enlightenment or Age of Reason if you will, a new technological era of productivity, creativity, and abundance unprecedented in human history. This new age will be brought about by a revitalized private sector as the public grows more and more disillusioned with political solutions (which never work) to social problems.

Yes, a new technology is currently being developed by private initiative, a technology which will render obsolete the arguments traditionally used for the "necessity" of welfare state reforms. Private industry is now rising to fill the vacuum created by the failures of socialism, not only in the United States, but in western Europe and eventually throughout the world. I take the view that George Orwell's scenario for 1984 will not come to pass.

We owe him a great debt for warning us against the horrors of a worldwide dictatorship, and the model he created is one that should never be forgotten.

But, I say again, it will not happen.

It is worthwhile taking a look at some of the original goals of the Social Democrats, and the profoundly pessimistic view of human nature they were based on. By analyzing the failure of socialism and welfare-state liberalism to bring us anything like the Utopia its advocates envisioned a half-century back, we will have a better understanding of why it is in a state of general collapse today—and why the creativity of the marketplace is erupting once again to bring us an era of prosperity and abundance.

11

The Piecemeal Approach to Socialism

1

American liberalism did not spring up overnight with the advent of Franklin Delano Roosevelt and his New Deal. Its roots go back to the American progressive era and the European social democratic movement which had already surfaced in Germany before the turn of the twentieth century, and later spread to Russia and much of western Europe by the time the United States was girding itself for World War I. The rhetoric was changed by the time the New Dealers adapted the ideas to the American system; indeed, most liberals have tended to think of themselves more as reform capitalists than as social democrats or democratic socialists like their European counterparts. They are concerned about "making capitalism work better," making it more "humane and responsive to the public interest," rather than with ushering in the socialist millennium. I have no doubt that much of the liberal rank-and-file, and some of its political leadership, have come to accept this rhetoric on its face value. In an age when many of us can't seem to remember what happened beyond last night's Tonight Show, it is insensitive to fault people for historical myopia. But the intellectual leadership of the liberal left, the ideologues who set the tone for a movement over the long run, have been avowedly socialist all along, and have been calling for liberals to abandon their reform-capitalist rhetoric in favor of an open socialist position.

"I am a democratic socialist," says Nat Hentoff, author and columnist for the *Village Voice*. "Capitalism, even the mixed capitalism that exists today, is impossible to justify if life is to be sustained and regenerated. . . . This country must begin to develop that human-service, socialistic society whose citizens, under political democracy, act in free will for their own best interests and those of the rest of the world."

John Kenneth Galbraith (whom I have always regarded as a fair novelist, but a less successful nonfiction writer), a long-time critic of capitalism and proponent of democratic socialism, is regarded as the high priest of economic affairs by even the more moderate liberal politicians—those constituting the "soft center" of American politics, as Norman Mailer puts it.

One by one, the intellectuals of the left put themselves firmly in the socialist camp. Gloria Steinem, Jack Newfield, Max Lerner, Paul Kurtz, Margaret Mead, Noam Chomsky, Christopher Lasch, Michael Harrington, Norman Cousins—those who may be considered the trendsetters of left-wing politics in America—have jettisoned the rhetoric of mixed-economy capitalism in favor of undiluted socialism. They attribute the failures of liberalism to the elements of capitalism remaining in our economic system, *not* to any shortcomings in the socialistic reforms already achieved. They are all rather panicky over the fact that the American public is growing disillusioned with welfare state reforms—primarily because of an intolerable tax burden and a corresponding decline in the quality of governmental services—and, because of this, the pace-setters of the left dread a middle class exodus to the political right, toward capitalistic solutions to our social problems.

(You will note that any movement, however slight, in the direction of capitalism is labeled "middle-class backlash," while sheep-like obeisance to the dictates of socialist planners is considered "humanistic progress.")

Because of this mounting fear on the left, its intellectual wizards are determined to speed up the reel of history, to abolish the remnants of capitalism in our system and totally socialize the nation before the middle class becomes too *uppity*. They are determined to prove that *pure* socialism, as opposed to the hybrid capitalist-socialism they have already bestowed on the country, will work if allowed to rule unhampered. If they can find some way of eliminating all opposition to their utopian pipedream, they are convinced, they can save humanity from itself. It would be more "humane" to wipe out the opposition *democratically*, of course, through the electoral process. But some of this contingent, following the lead of Michael Harrington and his benevolent dictatorship, are no longer concerned about the niceties of constitutional democracy. The totalitarian liberals, as George Orwell described them in the late 1940s, are coming out of the closet with all their warts exposed. In desperation they have decided, what the hell, it's time to take off the gloves and slap some sense into reactionary fascists who still believe in private property and the profit motive. If they refuse to listen to *reason* and vote for progressive reforms, then . . . well, what else can you do when the survival of humanity is at stake?

To be sure, people like Hentoff and Steinem remain committed to the *democratic* part of their socialist politics. But in the wings are the Michael Harringtons, the

Marcuseans, the Doomsday Brigade, the World Federalists, and others whose voices grow shriller every day. There are firmly entrenched members of the liberal establishment, like Rexford Guy Tugwell, who want to rewrite the United States Constitution and install a president (a liberal Democrat of course) for life; to give him more power so his will cannot be thwarted by the divisionary tactics of a recalcitrant congress. Yes, the voice of American liberalism grows more and more authoritarian, more dictatorial as the structure of New Deal, New Frontier, Great Society paternalism comes further apart at the seams. The socialist planners are custodians of a crumbling house, a house they know is rotting through to its very foundation, and they are determined to have one final go at it before watching it collapse forever.

I do not think they can salvage the wreck. I believe they have had their day and it is coming to an end. But then again, I am just an irresponsible optimist.

2

Progressivism. Social democracy. The New Deal. The piecemeal approach to socialism. Ideas, like flowers and poison ivy, all have roots somewhere. Modern liberalism in America can be traced to the progressive era which first began to take form in the years following the Civil War. Progressivism was an amorphous ideology, a hybrid blend of folksy American populism and "social realism." The word *ideology* is actually misplaced here, since the movement was more firmly rooted in vague sentimentality than it was in intellectual diligence. The older progressives were really neo-laissez faire types advocating a return to a more competitive decentralized marketplace which had already been destroyed by extensive federal intervention in the economy. But these were a minority. The larger factions wanted no part of Jeffersonian individualism; they called, instead, for a "new order," for "stronger organization and stability" in American life—

particularly American economic life. Their rhetoric was not altogether different from contemporary liberal sloganeering. It was heavily weighted with ringing demands for "rational central planning," "the creation of a decision-making mechanism in the federal government," and "immediate social reforms to prevent chaos."

Everywhere, the novelists and journalists of the period were discovering social obligations. The intellectuals, who regarded themselves as second-class citizens in a country dominated by businessmen and industrialists, lost no time in jumping aboard the progressive bandwagon. Now it was their turn to seek revenge for generations of neglect and denial. In past centuries the wisest kings knew enough to pamper the intellectuals; to give them top billing over the court jesters; to toss them a few scraps of prime meat to assuage their hunger pangs and feed their delicate egos. But America, during its first hundred years, was too busy civilizing a continent and enjoying the benefits of a free economy to pay much attention to its artists and writers, and there was no Eric Hoffer around at the time to analyze the latent bitchiness of a frustrated intelligentsia. So the progressive movement provided the intellectuals with just the outlet they were looking for. In droves they enlisted in the army of social engineers whose prime purpose was to enact social change through the rational persuasion of a strong central government.

3

The basic creed of progressivism is best summed up in Herbert Croley's *The Promise of American Life* (published in 1909), which became the political bible for writers like John Dewey, Walter Lippmann, Jane Addams, Van Wyck Brooks, Randolph Bourne, Charles Beard, George Soule, Bruce Bliven, and others who constituted the "voice of the *New Republic*" after 1914. Croley's program called for a steady march toward democratic collectivism in the economic, social, and cultural life of the country. The nation could no longer afford the ethic of competition and private gain, said Croley. The "Promise of American Life" would be fulfilled, "not by . . . economic freedom, but by a certain measure of discipline; not by the abundant satisfaction of individual desires, but by a large measure of individual subordination and self-denial." Croley specifically recommended an acceptance of economic and political centralization as the best means of organizing a modern society, particularly the regulation of large corporations in the public interest. He also proposed the use of progressive taxation to redistribute wealth and profits. Herbert Croley did not consider himself a socialist, preferring the label "mixed-economy progressive."

Strongly influenced by Croley's ideas, Van Wyck Brooks published a series of widely-read articles in various journals from 1915 through 1917 directed primarily at writers, journalists, and other architects of public opinion. He declared it was time for intellectuals to assert themselves and start devoting their talents to the achievement of social reforms (Intellectuals of the world, unite! You have nothing to lose but your anonymity!). His writings reflected an open antipathy for businessmen, and he excoriated them for alienating intellectuals from American life. Van Wyck Brooks diagnosed the central disease of the time as "insane individualism," "a historic obsession with self-reliance and personal achievement." He was especially bilious toward other writers linked with "the enemy camp," particularly Nathaniel Hawthorne and Mark Twain, who had been "seduced by the ethic of individualism." Unlike Croley, Brooks used the word *socialist* to describe his own political orientation, thereby advancing this indigenous American movement a step closer toward the European tradition.

American-style progressivism suffered a devastating blow in the wake of World War I. The public was too busy finding release for the bottled-up frenzy of the war years, and the entire mood of the nation drifted away from social consciousness toward the footloose hedonism that characterized the 1920s. Indeed, the entire left wing in America was in disarray during this period. The Socialist Party, which had its roots in European social democracy, and the IWW, which espoused a Bakuninist style of syndicalism, had both failed to make significant inroads into the American trade labor unions. The left wing was left with a loose coalition of radicals and liberals—the radicals oriented more toward European socialism; the liberals more toward American progressivism—all of whom were more or less influenced by Karl Marx. The progressive movement had a final fling in the 1924 presidential campaign of Robert La Follette, but its momentum as an autonomous movement separate and distinct from European socialism was already spent. In America during the late 1920s the radicals (socialists) began putting more and more pressure on liberals (progressives) to move further to the left, to abandon the rhetoric of reform capitalism in favor of unadulterated socialism.

With both groups on the ropes, staggering from the rampant lack of concern for social issues during the 1920s, it was inevitable that a merger of sorts would be forged between these two broad left-wing camps. There was power in numbers, and only a more closely-knit coalition could provide the left with the manpower necessary to launch a viable political movement in the United States.

A coalition and a catalyst. The coalition was already taking place in the twilight days of the 1920s. The catalyst was to be provided by the crash of the American stock market in 1929.

4

The great irony of the presidential campaign of 1932 is that Franklin Delano Roosevelt was actually elected as the more conservative of the two candidates. Repeatedly throughout the campaign, FDR denounced Herbert Hoover for deficit spending and he vowed to roll back taxes by a fixed amount each year—sometimes referring to across-the-board tax cuts in the 25 percent range. His fundamental campaign theme was economy in government, which had strong appeal among the nation's farmers and midwestern merchants. He rebuked Hoover for his "arm-twisting method" of slowing inflation and stabilizing the economy, and accused him of concentrating too much power in the hands of federal planners.

According to FDR's closest advisers at the time, their presidential candidate was basically unprincipled and untutored ideologically. Heywood Broun described him in 1932 as "the corkscrew candidate of a convoluting convention," meaning that he was willing to bend and twist himself in any direction to present himself as all things to all people. Leading reporters assigned to FDR's campaign portrayed him as an amiable and ambitious but incompetent and wobbly governor who was dangerous because of both his lack of experience and his blatant political opportunism. If he had a real program of his own designed to pull the country out of the depression, it lay so well concealed in his mind that not even his closest associates were aware of it. During this election year Walter Lippmann, a thoroughgoing progressive, observed that the governor of New York had no discernible qualifications for the presidency other than an obvious ambition. On the other hand, Herbert Hoover had already established impeccable liberal credentials during World War I as Food Organizer in the Wilson administration. Progressive Democrats had unsuccessfully attempted to draft him as their party's presidential candidate in 1920.

The most revealing insight into the mind of FDR in campaign year 1932 comes from Rexford Guy Tugwell, a leading member of the so-called Brain Trust and, along with Adolph A. Berle, the most important architect of the New Deal. He served as undersecretary of agriculture from 1933 to 1937. In his book *In Search of Roosevelt*, Tugwell takes a pompous self-righteous pride in having "educated" FDR in the virtues of collectivism:

> Roosevelt knew only a little about the competing ideas seething then in the less formal literature of the social sciences. My specialty, if I had one, was the study of social invention—especially, of course, in economic life. I had always been enormously interested in the creative intelligence—how things were made and ideas shaped, how novelty was possible and where it came from. And I had a good deal of work behind me; but not more than Adolph Berle, who was my junior by several years but had been a prodigy of early learning.

The cloying smugness, the mock humility and ravenous appetite for ego gratification exhibited in this passage are typical of just about all of Tugwell's writing. He is just too-too precious on the surface to be all that humanistic underneath. Yet his intellectual influence on FDR was enormous, and has been amply corroborated by other writers of the period. Throughout his book Tugwell refers to FDR's "flypaper mind"—just perfect, of course, for snapping up whatever morsels of wisdom Tugwell and the Brain Trusters decided to toss at it.

And what of Tugwell's ideological makeup? In his own words, he and Adolph Berle were called "Reds, Communists, Socialists, Anarchists, and even, on occasion, Fascists." The only label he would accept, however, was "Collectivists," which more generally described the pattern of their ideas. Tugwell, Raymond Moley, and Adolph Berle shaped an economic program for FDR which they described as "concentration and control . . . based on coordination or collectivism as over against individualism and atomism [i.e., competition]."

As self-avowed collectivists, they openly admired Benito Mussolini's fascist plan for revitalizing the Italian economy. They scoffed at natural law theory and free economic competition, and argued for large state-controlled corporations in the fascist model, thereby dispelling the myth that the New Deal was created to *break up* monopoly capitalism. Tugwell kept pressing on FDR the notion that the free market of Adam Smith was gone forever, and he urged him to accept the inevitability of state-run monopolies as the most efficient means of organizing the American economy. Tugwell and Berle repeatedly argued against decentralizing the economy and returning to a competitive, "atomistic" system. Tugwell, more so than Berle, Moley, and Lippmann, despised the business community and wanted it totally managed by the federal government in a joint government-corporate partnership. By the time the election of 1932 rolled around, Tugwell was able to boast: "[FDR] had made himself into a good deal of a collectivist and was reconciled to the inevitability of large-scale organization; he had a beginning of faith in economic planning. . . ."

5

Franklin Delano Roosevelt performed a complete turnabout after his inauguration in the spring of 1933. The man who had accused Herbert Hoover of arm-twisting and economic tyranny in his own administration suddenly asked for broad executive power to wage a war against the national emergency, "as great as the power that would be given to me if we were in fact invaded by a foreign foe." What if congress failed to bend to the new president's will? The whole country must rise up against the legislative branch with a demand for universal sacrifice, discipline, and strong federal action.

FDR and his Brain Trusters were not the only ones flirting with the concept of a temporary benevolent dictatorship to deal with the national crisis. Mussolini's success in Italy had not gone unnoticed by the news media, especially the humanitarian liberals at the *New York*

Times. As Ann O'Hare McCormick, a reporter for that freedom-loving organ, wrote in 1933: "The atmosphere [in Washington at the beginning of the New Deal] is strangely reminiscent of Rome in the first weeks after the march of the Blackshirts, of Moscow at the beginning of the Five-Year Plan. . . . The new capitol built by Mr. Hoover presupposes just such a highly centralized, all-inclusive government as is now in the making."

McCormick, writing in praise of FDR and the New Deal, euphorically described Washington, D.C., Rome, and Moscow as the great "revolutionary capitals" of the time.

She continued: ". . . something far more positive than acquiescence vests the President with the authority of a dictator. This authority is a free gift, a sort of unanimous power of attorney. . . . America today literally asks for orders. . . . Not only does the present occupant of the White House possess more authority than any of his predecessors, but he presides over a government that has more control over more private activities than any other that has ever existed in the United States. . . . [The FDR administration] envisions a federation of industry, labor, and government after the fashion of the corporate state as it exists in Italy."

Lest you think the notion of one-world dictatorship is relatively new, this also flowed from the pen of the same lady: "[FDR] has dramatically placed himself at the head of the world. He does not ask for a mandate as an international dictator, welcome as such a governor might be to a distracted planet, but if he gets the authority he wants from Congress . . . he would be in position to exercise almost as much power abroad as he wields at home. . . . Nobody is much disturbed by the idea of dictatorship. Mr. Roosevelt does not fit into the popular conception of a dictator, and there is a general feeling that he collects powers as he collects opinions—to be ready for emergencies rather than with the intention of using them. . . . Here is a new kind of rule—what might be described as the permissive dictatorship, evolved in a few weeks by a concert of powers: the President, the people, the tyranny of events."

All the above is lifted from the *New York Times Magazine* of May 7, 1933—the publication which publishes all the news fit to print.

So we see that the liberal left has evolved from the permissive dictatorship of Ann O'Hare McCormick to the temporary benevolent dictatorship of Michael Harrington, presented but of course in the most hypnotically humanistic jargon yet devised by a human brain. How coy, how sugar-sweet. But what dangerous and horrendous rubbish it all is. The same mentality which referred to Rose Kennedy as "the closest thing America has to a Queen Mother" in 1962 would no doubt have installed Eleanor Roosevelt as Queen of all the Americas, yea the very length and breadth of the planet, if given the opportunity in 1933. From a Rooseveltian Empire in 1933 to Camelot in 1961—in one delicate bounce. Adolph Berle was not joshing in 1932 when he called the New Deal "the Social Gospel of creating a Kingdom of God on Earth"; nor Arthur Schlesinger in later years when he claimed FDR believed "he walked with God, that he was the instrument of the Lord, and that the Lord would care for him in moments of trial."

No, the divine right of kings did not end with the fall of monarchies. It existed at the beginning of the New Deal, and it exists among us today in the thinking of many American liberals. This divine right of rule, however, is not transferable to Republican presidents. The Lord God Almighty, you see, is a registered Democrat.

6

Common Sense, an important left-wing magazine of the period (the title of which was rather blasphemously expropriated from Thomas Paine), heralded the FDR administration as "the official end of laissez faire and nineteenth-century individualism [although, as we have seen, laissez-faire economics was already on the wane in the final years of the last century]." The New Deal, according to the *Nation*, was "a promising first step toward a collectivized society with a strong labor movement and fundamental redistribution of wealth." In late 1932, following Roosevelt's victory, the *Nation* had published a list of suggestions for the president-elect. Among them were: firm government control of production and wages; massive public works projects; nationalization of banks and the mass transportation industries; a concerted federal attack on the ethic of private profit and economic competition. Roosevelt, having learned his lessons well at the collective feet of Tugwell and Berle, promised to launch a program of government-industry cooperation (i.e., a government-managed economy); distribute massive relief funds to farmers and small merchants; accept responsibility for the welfare of millions of unemployed; inaugurate a program of far-ranging experimentation in central planning (a la Russia's Five-Year Plan); establish large public works projects; guarantee bank deposits with federal tax dollars; and regulate the brokerage houses on Wall Street.

Ideologically, all these programs translated into a grab-bag philosophy of American progressivism, grass-roots populism, Italian fascism, *mittel*-European democratic socialism, and urban social reformism in the Jane Addams-John Dewey mold—a collectivist stew of sorts. The far left in the United States, composed of doctrinaire socialists and Marxists, was a bit uneasy over the fact that FDR was modeling his New Deal too closely on Mussolini's corporate state to suit its own tastes. It preferred that Roosevelt steer the nation in a more consistently Marxist direction, and kept up a steady pressure on his administration throughout the decade to move further to the left. But, for the moment, the socialist-communist wing of the American left had little choice but to align itself with the New Deal Democrats. There simply was no other ballgame in town at the time. At least the new president was a collectivist, however impure, and sooner or later he might be guided onto the straight and narrow Marxist road.

The most important job for the American left in the early days of the Roosevelt administration was the creation of a Popular Front, a broad coalition of dissident classes and groups, to engage in a long struggle for social change. The ultimate goal would be to push the country far beyond the New Deal toward an indigenous form of socialism. George Soule, in his book, *The Coming American Revolution* (published in 1934), warned the far left against indulging in any Leninist fantasies. The European design of fomenting social upheavals with rioting mobs, violent class conflicts, dramatic assaults on the government, and a convulsive overthrow of the old order would not succeed in America, Soule claimed. The American public was basically too conservative, too indoctrinated by a century and a half of capitalist individualism to respond to the bugle call of a Marxist revolution. "A true revolution [in the United States] would take many years, even generations in the making." The proper course for the American left was to "work through the New Deal" to fuse all disparate classes and elements into a new social order.

(In effect, he was calling for the piecemeal approach to socialism as espoused by European social democrats, a kind of Chinese water torture approach to socialism; drop by drop it breaks down your will to resist over the long run.)

This, of course, was the old argument between the Mensheviks and Bolsheviks resurrected for the American situation—an argument that divided radical communists and moderate socialists in the Internationale in the late nineteenth century. Soule advocated a gradual, systematic "control of production, prices, wages, investments, and purchasing power," all of which would add up to socialism over a period of time. He felt that a rigorous implementation of Keynesian economics in the United States was "by nature antagonistic to the basic requirements of capitalism," and therefore ought to be encouraged. He was confident that, as capitalism was progressively eroded by New Deal reforms, a genuine socialist party would emerge to seize power.

"Capitalism must in the end give way to the rise of the working classes and socialism."

7

Political. Economic. Social. Cultural. Ideological. The struggle would continue for years on all fronts. Whether the orthodox Marxists in the United States were persuaded by the power of Soule's impeccable logic, or they simply accepted the reality of the American condition, is difficult to say. But Soule, perhaps more than any other voice of the time, succeeded in muting the far-left call for "violent social upheaval." Louis Fraina, a pseudonym for Lewis Corey, who was one of the founders of the American Communist Party in 1919, agreed that the situation in the United States was indeed unique, and he committed himself to Soule's piecemeal approach to socialism. In his view, the left should work in tandem to "proletarianize" the American middle class. This would be accomplished by a steady application of New Deal reforms designed to weaken the capitalist economy and "create crises"—crises which "only socialist programs" could solve. Other writers joined Soule and Fraina in recognizing that the only way to bring socialism to the United States was through reform within the system, and especially by working with the Democratic Party, since the great majority of Americans would never openly support a left-wing fringe party.

The *Nation* and *New Republic* quickly began calling for a "revitalized Democratic Party" of the broadest scope, encompassing all those forces—farmers, Negroes, clerks, salesmen, small businessmen, teachers, engineers, white collar professionals, managers, intellectuals, and industrial workers—"which can be made to see their interest in the abolition of capitalism." This popular front party would "Americanize Karl Marx" by emphasizing piecemeal, democratic reforms instead of a proletarian revolution. The New Deal, of course, would be the instrument of these reforms. The Democratic Party would dedicate itself to "a planned cooperative commonwealth, with public ownership of the basic means of production."

The *New Republic* was particularly adroit at performing this ideological balancing act. Under the intellectual guidance of writers like Bruce Bliven, George Soule, Edmund Wilson, Malcolm Cowley, John Dewey, Stuart Chase, Rexford Guy Tugwell, and Lewis Mumford, the magazine managed to keep its philosophical feet firmly in both the liberal (reform capitalist) and radical (socialist) camps. The *Nation*, under the editorship of Oswald Garrison Villard, featured Max Lerner and Freda Kirschner on political and social issues, and published articles by Granville Hicks, Sidney Hook, Philip Rahv, Lionel Trilling, and others. Both these journals, together with *Common Sense*, *Social Frontier*, and the Communist organs *New Masses* and the *Daily Worker*, were euphoric about the prospects of forging a popular front on the left to launch the socialist millennium. Their overall policy was to urge Roosevelt gradually to the left, toward a genuine socialist ideology that was indigenous to the United States.

Max Lerner, Archibald MacLeish, and Corliss Lamont stressed the compatibility between liberalism and socialism. Both camps, they argued, were committed to scientific methods in solving social problems. What was class struggle if not a synonym for the more euphemistic term, *political action by enlightened persuasion?* Lerner and Frederich Schuman even went so far as to state that democratic socialism was the ultimate goal of Marxism—which must have come as quite a shock to the more dogmatic Marxists who assumed their ultimate goal was a worldwide factory full of contented workers bending to their tasks in an atmosphere of voluntary slavery. Then again, the liberals have never been subtle in their efforts to co-opt the hairier fringes on the left. Lerner and Schuman both wanted a liberal-Communist alliance which would "produce a new philosophical synthesis, combining the best strains of Marxism and pragmatism. . . ." In less grandiose terms, this meant turning both Marxism and progressivism into an American form of democratic socialism, a nice feat if Messrs Lerner and Schuman could pull it off.

Edmund Wilson also lent his talents to this philosophical synthesis movement, formulating the concept of "translating Marxism into terms most Americans could understand." The basic assumption behind all of it was that a socialist society could be built by imposing a welfare state on top of a state-controlled economy which, through piecemeal reforms, would erode the remaining vestiges of capitalism in America. It was as though the liberals envisioned themselves in the role of philosophical geneticists, hoping to create a hybrid strain of socialism through a series of ideological mutations. American-style socialism would not be unadulterated Marxism, but rather a more durable indigenous version forged in the intellectual laboratories of the liberal press.

8

But it was not to come off according to plan. The reason for this was simple and practical: FDR's New Deal measures did not succeed in stimulating the economy; quite the reverse. National income in 1934 was ten billion dollars less than in 1931, and only half that of 1929. In the fall of 1934 unemployment stood at roughly the same level as it had two years earlier. Harry Hopkins, a former New York social worker under Governor Roosevelt who was described by Robert Sherwood as the most powerful man in Roosevelt's administration from the middle-1930s right through to the war years, confided in 1934: "Nobody seems to think anymore that the thing [the New Deal] is going to work." But the worse the American economic situation became, the more adamant Hopkins was about imposing new and more drastic reforms on the economy. "Boys—this is our hour," he said. "We've got to get everything we want—a works program, social security, wages and hours, everything—now or never."

Responding to strong pressure from the left, Hopkins spent five million dollars in his first two hours in office. Critics of the New Deal accused Hopkins of spending the taxpayers' money "like a Medici Prince." With each new failure he urged additional programs on FDR, pushing him ever leftward. He put four-and-a-quarter million people to work for the Civil Works Administration, as many as had served in the armed forces during World War I. Artists, writers, opera singers, archeologists, day laborers, and everyone else he could lay his hands on were given a federal paycheck. Where all the money for public salaries was going to come from if he succeeded in totally destroying the private sector did not seem to concern him. He was like a Bowery bum suddenly turned loose in the vaults of Chase Manhattan Bank; a sailor locked up overnight inside a waterfront ginmill. There was simply no stopping the man in his obsession for depleting the public till.

Roosevelt himself began to grow panicky over the cost of Hopkins' "humanistic exuberance," and publicly expressed concern that he was creating a permanent class of reliefers whom he might never be able to separate from the public dole. This attitude, however, is further evidence of FDR's lack of ideological sophistication. He never fully grasped the idea that Hopkins, Tugwell, Moley, Berle and company were not concerned about *ever* diminishing the growing army of public reliefers and employees. It was their intention from the start to turn virtually the entire American work force into public employees by collectivizing, if not actually nationalizing, the major industries. FDR's wife Eleanor had a much clearer grasp of the true purpose of the New Deal, and was the real ideologue in the family. *La Boca Grande*, as Westbrook Pegler labeled the Queen Mother of the American Left in the 1940s, served as a kind of ideological shield between the Brain Trusters and her husband lest he grow gun-shy over their left-wing sloganeering. Her job was to "strain" the rhetoric and spoonfeed it to him like pablum. In many ways the old booby was an old-fashioned American patriot at heart—a willing dupe of the collectivists, however, because of his ravenous appetite for more and more power.

9

A temporary upswing in the economy, combined with an ineffectual Republican presidential campaign, put Roosevelt back in office for a second term in 1936. But, less than a year later, the unemployment rolls had swollen to 1932 levels once again, and the newspapers of the country were filled with reports about "roving bands of children salvaging food from garbage cans, families fighting one another for spoiled food dumped in the streets near markets, and a marked increase in the suicide rate among the unemployed." Harry Hopkins, the intrepid social worker himself, admitted that starvation was widespread in seventeen southern states and other areas throughout the country. The WPA (Works Progress Administration) could not put anyone else to work because of lack of funds, and relief treasuries were in a state of bankruptcy. A number of social critics, including Bernard De Voto and Hugh Johnson, wrote articles and books claiming that the current depression was worse than Herbert Hoover's. The off-year elections of 1938 put many conservatives back in congress who, together with disaffiliated Democrats, formed a bipartisan bloc to stymie additional New Deal measures. Even Raymond Moley, the organizer of the Brain Trust, was forced to admit: "It looks as though the majority of those over 45 probably will never get their jobs back."

The greatest tragedy of the time was the fact that the hard-core intelligentsia refused to acknowledge the failure of New Deal legislation to end the depression, and continued to argue for a purer form of socialism. Possibly, the main reason for this can be attributed to the unprecedented power and influence the intellectuals were enjoying in America through the Roosevelt administration. Anyone with the ability to wield a paint brush and slap a little paint against a canvas, or the presence of mind to tap out a semiliterate poem dripping with "social realism," was guaranteed a public paycheck. The talented, near-talented, and sycophantic untalented were all given refuge under the federal umbrella. The intellectuals who refused to go along with the collectivist hysteria sweeping the nation—true men and women of genius like H. L. Mencken, Albert Jay Nock, and Rose Wilder Lane, unrepentent individualists to the last—would never regain the stature they had known in the 1920s. Nowhere else, except in Soviet Russia, was the "socially relevant" artist and writer treated with so much respect. Overlooked was the fact that Russian writers had, in effect, been drafted into the service of the state. They were pampered and fed just so long as they kept their noses clean and spewed out party-line propaganda. Official subsidization brought with it a corresponding loss of artistic freedom. No matter, though. It is easy to overlook the more distasteful facts when the meals are steady and the rent bill is being taken care of. Prostitution, like benevolence and beauty, is also in the eye of the beholder.

Of particular interest is the silence of American left-wing intellectuals during the Stalin purge trials from 1935 through 1938. Many of them admitted being "confused" by Stalin's violence (Boy, is he *strict*!), but notable authors like Malcolm Cowley, Dashiell Hammett, Lillian Hellman, Langston Hughes, Dorothy Parker, Henry Roth, and Irwin Shaw defended his massive bloodbath in a joint declaration published in the *New Masses* on May 3, 1938. Anti-Stalinist critics denigrated the left for tolerating political repression in Russia while automatically denouncing abridgement of freedom in the United States. Defending itself against this charge, the *New Republic* replied: ". . . civil liberties are never absolute, and free thought and judicial safeguards are always relative to the nature and aims of a particular social order." With this perspective, the editors found it easy to distinguish between dictatorship in the Soviet Union and Nazi totalitarianism in Germany. In the U.S.S.R. the ultimate goal was the creation of a "classless society," whereas Germany's social gospel was nothing more than "racial mythology." In other words, government can do *anything at all* if its heart is in the right place.

If the editorial position of the *New Republic* at the time sounds a trifle swinish, it was really quite moderate compared to other views. Louis Fischer went so far as to say that "political coercion is perfectly permissible for a government [read socialist government] to protect itself," thereby qualifying himself as the Herbert Marcuse of his day. Frederich Schuman praised Stalin during the Moscow trials as a "steeled organizer and activist" who knew how to deal with practical problems quickly and efficiently.

There is nothing quite so efficient as a steeled Communist dictator, to be sure.

10

What was responsible for the failure of the New Deal to end the depression? Certainly not the quasisocialist nature of the reforms themselves. If anything, according to popular front intellectuals, Roosevelt had *not gone far enough*. He was not a consistent socialist. Since FDR's welfare state approach had failed to end hunger and poverty, reduce unemployment, and restore prosperity, the only logical alternative was to move more dramatically toward socialism, to speed up the evolutionary cycle so to speak and bring the revolution to America ahead of schedule. Rexford Guy Tugwell, who certainly knows how to twist a syllogism along with the best of them, put the blame on Roosevelt's vacillation between collectivism and individualism—the element of capitalism remaining in his reforms because of FDR's "cautious and halfhearted approaches." Roosevelt, you see, simply did not go far enough in collectivizing the economy.

But whatever rationalizations the New Deal apologists were able to muster, there was no denying the simple facts: the economy was, if anything, in worse shape than when FDR took office. The American work force was top-heavy with unskilled labor and suffered from a severe shortage of skilled labor. Ironically enough, hundreds of thousands of jobs were going begging for lack of qualified applicants while the unemployment rolls continued to hover at a catastrophic level. Public treasuries, both state and federal, were bankrupt and FDR's promised relief checks failed to go out on time or evaporated altogether.

By 1938 much of FDR's support was severely splintered. The divisions among liberals, socialists, Communists, Trotskyites—a mind-boggling array of factions within factions—grew wider once again, and the popular front literally started to come undone at the joints. FDR's army of intellectuals, no doubt growing a bit miffed over the direction their utopian pipedream had taken, began to drop out of politics in favor of cultural pursuits. Here they had consented to dirty their hands in the political soil to rebuild America, and the piggish American public had failed to lend a hand like good proletarians ought to. Well, to hell with that. The American citizenry had its chance and blew it. Writers like Dwight Macdonald announced they would henceforth dedicate themselves solely to the Muse. Let the public eat its collective heart out.

Others bolted to the political right, claiming they had learned to treasure freedom above everything else. "The dictators have taught us to love freedom more," Louis Fischer declared in 1939. By the time the war broke out in Europe, the coloration of left-wing ideology was more anti-fascist than it was pro-anything else. The Hitler-Stalin pact disillusioned many American intellectuals about the virtues of collectivism (in any form). Individualism would experience a renaissance of sorts through the efforts of the perennial H. L. Mencken, Frank Chodorov, Rose Wilder Lane, Isabel Paterson, Garet Garrett, and other writers who had never been swept up by the New Deal euphoria to begin with. Less political writers began to attack the concept of a centrally-planned society, whether modeled on socialism, fascism, or welfarism. William Saroyan remarked that the 1930s taught the artist an invaluable lesson: that he must elude every attempt at external coercion, that he is inescapably a "dweller in an ivory tower" for whom "historical action was out of the question."

Henry Miller was even more to the point: "Society is made up entirely of individuals, not groups or classes. Consequently each single man should try to rise above the crowd . . . repudiating all gods and leaders, recognizing instead that the solitary individual must work with his own hands to save himself." Miller's path was to "turn his gaze inward, contemplating his private fate with awe and wonder, mystery and reverence, inventing his own miracles, wreaking his own havoc, in a universe bereft of revolutionary visions and utopian dreams."

And Ernest Hemingway, who had been denounced in the middle-1930s for refusing to join the Communist Party, was most succinct of all. "Ideology," said the master, "is no substitute for art." He went on to describe himself as an individualist above everything else, a man who did not believe in burying his individuality in the cause of collectivizing mankind. His personal *bete noir* was the high level of taxation which ate away a good percentage of his earning power.

American-style socialism, quite simply, was costing him too much money.

11

And so we come to Camelot. From *La Boca Grande* to Mother Rose, "the closest thing America has to a Queen Mother." God save us all from the divine right of Democratic presidents. And we come, of course, to President JFK (the liberals like initials with a trinitarian ring to them), Queen Jackie before she became enchanted with the olive groves of Greece, and the New Frontier mandarins of 1960. The intellectuals had to suffer through a twenty-year hiatus before discovering another philosopher-king to build a new social gospel around. This one was young, athletic, and goodlooking—much more charismatic than his predecessor in the role. It was almost as though he had been grown specially to order by a New Deal geneticist, some liberal biochemist with a monopoly on Brave New World technology. And what about that First Lady of his? Where *La Boca Grande* had just that right touch of frumpy domineering maternalism about her, the new queen was tailor-made for the jet age with its emphasis on eternal youth and supersonic movement. The euphoria surrounding the New Frontier administration of 1960 was on a par with that of twenty-eight years earlier, although, so far as I recall, there were no explicit calls for dictatorship in the *New York Times* or any other major publication. The editorialists, apparently, had missed their cue.

So much has been written about the similarities between the 1930s and the 1960s that one hesitates to belabor the obvious. The similarities are there, to be sure, but the differences significantly outweigh the similarities. It was these very differences that made it much less likely the left would succeed in implanting socialism on American society in the 1960s—differences which have been overlooked, for the most part, by the press in its attempts to emphasize the continuity of New Deal, New Frontier, Great Society reforms.

12

But first, the similarities. As in 1932 the mass exodus of intellectuals, particularly academicians, from the universities to the nation's capital. The army of experts and social engineers with three and six and nine letters after their names marching off to Washington to participate in the great new experiment in social and economic planning. Their rhetoric was remarkably similar to that of FDR's New Dealers; there was no reason why it shouldn't be, since the basic ideas were no more than an amalgam of retread socialism, welfarism, and mixed-economy collectivism. Nothing substantially new had been added to the stew in thirty years. The Kennedy intellectuals hyped up the ideas with a few new labels, perhaps, but their basic message was virtually identical to that of Tugwell and the Brain Trusters.

Second—the lineup in the wings. The fuzzy fringe brigade of socialists and Communists was given an added dash of color by Maoists after the Chinese model, Castroites after the Cuban design, and, later on, Black Power Marxists a la the Black Panthers and anarcho-collectivists who had apparently fused together an ideology with drugs, sex, bluejeans, and the occult mysteries. Once again the far left would be enticed out of the closet by the charismatic allure of Washington, D.C., and would urge JFK and his mandarins to strip completely and take the full plunge into the murky waters of undiluted Marxism.

Then there was the same willingness to whitewash (if not enthusiastically endorse) Communist dictatorships in China and Cuba particularly, while sniffing self-righteously over violations of civil liberties under right-wing regimes in Spain, Greece, South Africa, and elsewhere. It is incredible to listen to the old 1930s rhetoric dressed up in 1960s jargon; the same sad, sorry babblings regurgitated in a subcultural youth slang. The left suffers from a chronic inability to learn the lessons of history and this, ultimately, will prove its final undoing. Contemporary leftists should read Karl Marx more thoroughly in this regard.

What else? Oh yes. By the late 1960s the left wing would be severely splintered once again, as it was in the late thirties following the disintegration of the Popular Front. In recent times the fringe elements abandoned politics in favor of "the environment," having developed a proprietary interest in trees, lakes, and rattlesnakes as though they had invented nature themselves, whereas thirty years earlier the left jettisoned politics after having rediscovered "culture." This mass retreat on the left from the political arena to cultural and environmental pursuits is an especially startling similarity between the two decades; it makes one toy with the cyclic theory of history (events replay themselves every other generation or so).

The final major similarity between the 1930s and the 1960s is the attempt to "reconstruct a consistent, cohesive ideology" acceptable to all elements on the left—an attempt which continues today without any apparent success. After World War II, right through the 1950s, the left underwent a process of soul-searching in a major effort to synthesize a consistent ideology from the various strains of prevalent left-wing thought. The warmed-over New Deal stew offered by both the JFK and Johnson administrations is evidence of the left's abysmal failure to do so. After twenty years of autoanalysis it could not produce anything more imaginative than the New Frontier-Great Society sloganeering of the early and middle-1960s. Today the left is even more fragmented than ever. Its competing ideologies have multiplied like rabbits over the years, with even orthodox Marxism broken down into a greater number of subcategories.

These, then, are the most significant similarities between the two decades. But they are surface similarities more than anything else. Down deep in the soul of the 1960s, down where the stirrings for change were taking place and the look of the future was shaping up, were abiding fundamental differences—overwhelming differences from the 1930s. These basic differences foreshadow the end of the socialist movement in the United States of America. They spell out the final collapse of collectivist thought, not only in America, but throughout much of the civilized world.

13

When Franklin Delano Roosevelt took office in 1933, American society was in as sorry a state as it had been since the War of Independence. One third of a nation, to use one of FDR's rallying cries, was poorly-clothed, poorly-housed, and poorly-fed. A massive percentage of the citizenry was desperate for solutions, *any kind* of solutions that would lift it out of the misery of the depression and restore an era of abundance and prosperity. The prospective "army of the left-wing revolution" was literally out there in the streets, scrounging through garbage cans for scraps of food, picking around in cluttered lots for the materials essential to the support of life. Conditions were perfect for the emergence of a socialist (or other type of collectivist) dictatorship. All the ingredients required for a successful takeover were present: a large body of poor and hungry people; general confusion over the proper direction to move in; a well-organized elite with a program for national recovery; a strong leader bent on power with the ability to galvanize the whole affair and put his grand design in motion.

The left wing in America had a once-in-a-lifetime

opportunity to revolutionize the country in the early 1930s and, to put it simply, it blew its golden hour. The left failed to exploit the *genuine* economic and social crises ripping apart the nation when it had the chance to do so. It failed primarily because collectivism in any form is incapable of rejuvenating a moribund economy; it is incapable of providing any society with a generally high standard of living; its history in every country where it has taken root is one of continuing failure and political slavery. Collectivism is a failure because it is, in its very fundamentals, a denial of human nature. It is based in a utopian dreamworld rather than the hard facts of reality. By suppressing individual differences and the drive for personal achievement, by attempting to equalize unequal human beings under the jackboot of political authoritarianism, socialists, welfarists, and fascists can only generate alienation and widespread discontent. If they do succeed in imposing an effective dictatorship over a society, they must of necessity create an apathetic citizenry unwilling to produce because of the lack of incentive to do so.

(Collectivism can work only if human nature is substantially altered. This is the insidious danger behind B. F. Skinner's behaviorist theories as outlined in *Beyond Freedom and Dignity*. More on this later.)

These facts are so elemental in understanding the human condition that it is truly a wonder how so many people continue to deny them. They simply *will* not accept reality. They are determined to refurbish human nature in their own image . . . or else destroy human society in their effort to do so.

Fortunately the New Dealers did not succeed in bringing socialism to America in the 1930s, and their chances of succeeding now grow slimmer every year. The social and economic conditions prevailing at the time are no longer with us. The ranks of the "proletariat" are decreasing steadily, and the left is running out of fodder for the socialist revolution.

14

By the time JFK took his oath of office the United States was already a predominantly middle-class country. Where one-third of the nation was going hungry in 1932, less than 10 percent was seriously malnourished in 1960—and the figure is under five percent today. The left wing has failed to absorb the fact that the American working class is irreversibly *middle class* in every conceivable area. The income of the average blue-collar worker is high enough to turn insurance executives green with envy. Policemen, firemen, tin knockers, and wire lathers live cheek-by-jowl with lawyers and doctors in choice suburban communities across the country; their children play on the same Little League teams together; to a great extent they dine out in the same expensive restaurants on weekends; and, according to the latest studies, they are even going to the same psychoanalysts. In the 1930s the main concern of the working class was feeding and clothing itself, while today its main interests are preserving a comfortable standard of living, combatting rising taxes and inflation, reducing crime and making our streets safe to walk in. As such, the American working class, including most of the union leadership, is committed to a private-property, private-enterprise system.

Quite simply, American "proletarians" are now card-carrying members of the *bourgeoisie*, thanks to the element of economic freedom the liberals have not been able to destroy.

Forty years ago the left had an even chance of forging a broad coalition with "farmers, Negroes, clerks, salesmen, small businessmen, teachers, engineers, white-collar professionals, managers, intellectuals, and industrial workers" because of the widespread discontent among all these groups. Today the socialists are left with blacks, Spanish-speaking immigrants, and (but of course) the humorless brigade of left-wing intellectuals and student revolutionaries. Most likely, by the time our landmark year of 1984 comes around, most blacks and chicanos will have worked their way into the middle class and the revolutionary coalition will have been reduced to a daisy chain consisting of university professors and editorial writers for the *New York Post*.

If the left is running out of revolutionary fodder, it is also growing short on *real* crises with which to galvanize the American public. Poverty and starvation were genuine issues in the days of FDR. Millions of people were literally homeless in the streets, cooking out over open fires and sleeping in makeshift huts. Today, notwithstanding Michael Harrington's attempt to stir public passions with his graphic account of "the other America," starvation in the United States has virtually been eliminated while the ranks of the poverty-stricken are a small fraction of what they were at the birth of the New Deal. The major concerns today are *high rents* rather than complete lack of housing, *inflation and rising taxes* rather than no income at all, and a *poorly-balanced diet* rather than massive shortages of food.

The much-publicized gap between rich and poor still exists, and will *always* exist in a free and relatively competitive society. Our comparative levels of achievement reflect our individual talents, personal drive, and capabilities in the marketplace. These differences are inherent in human nature and can be eradicated *only* by a dictatorship—and even then, a dictatorship of any sort can only succeed in reducing all of us to the level of the lowest common denominator. Overlooked in this *gap* school of socio-economic evangelism is the fact that the comparative levels of rich and poor have risen tremendously over the years; the poor live on a much higher level than they did in the past, and the number of the rich and comfortable in society has swollen while the number of poor has been on the decline.

As the left wing has been running out of genuine crises over the decades, it has been forced to *manufacture* new ones to justify its urgent call for socialist reforms. With hunger, poverty, and housing no longer monumental crises in American society, the left has turned to the environment for support. Hence, the advent of the Doomsday Brigade and its crusade for piecemeal socialism on a world scale. Having failed to convince the American public that its interests can best be served by socialism, the liberal-socialist-doomsday alliance has turned the spotlight on the international arena—the "world environment." Poverty, hunger, and inadequate housing do of course exist in places like India, Africa, and Asia. By lumping all these problems together under the heading *ecology*; by trying to convince the public that the *survival of the entire planet* is dependent on a wheat shortage in Pakistan, an oil spill in the Caspian Sea, or a drought in Pago Pago; by creating a *spaceship* theory out of our existence on earth (we are all passengers together on a dying space ship), the left will try to socialize the entire planet in a way it once hoped to collectivize the United States.

15

The left is destined to fail in this, for the same basic reasons it failed on a national level. It will fail because of three essential factors: the inherent inability of socialism (and collectivism in general) to solve crises; the elimination of ecological "crises" over a period of time in the same fashion socio-economic crises have virtually been eliminated in the United States; and a dwindling supply of convincing leadership.

To take up the last of these conditions first, the American electorate has had it clear up to its eyeballs with charismatic political leaders. The experience of John Lindsay as mayor of New York City was enough to send even his staunchest supporters back to the laboratories in search of a new kind of hero.

(Wavy hair, a pretty smile, and a low I.Q. do not a revolution make.)

In 1972 the American left tried—tried oh so hard and so self-righteously—to portray George McGovern as a latter-day Joan of Arc capable of bringing us the "Kingdom of God on Earth" in his first four-year term. What happened, instead, was that St. George turned out to be a political prostitute of the lowest rank, a tarnished street walker with an uncanny talent for selling his soul to the highest bidder in the grand old tradition of smoke-filled rooms and clubhouse deals.

This leaves the American left with a lineup of sad and tired old warhorses—used-up relics of the New Deal like Senators Hubert Humphrey and Henry "Scoop" Jackson. Both Jackson and George Wallace have appealed to some people on the political right because of their positions on law and order and foreign policy, but underneath the conservative-sounding rhetoric they are both New Deal Democrats with a taste for economic collectivism (and outright socialism in the case of "Scoop" Jackson). It was this latter gentleman who flirted with the notion of nationalizing the oil companies during the energy crisis of 1973. There is always the chance that the left will come up with a brand new demagogue by 1976, an engaging and persuasive dark horse capable of rallying the multitudes around a revitalized socialist bandwagon. But I do not think this will be the case. The American public grows more enlightened all the time; it has grown more wary over the tactics of political demagoguery; it has been stung too many times in the past.

As far as the first two factors are concerned, we have already discussed the failure of socialist reforms to solve the real crises of the depression of 1929, and there is no reason to think socialism will prove any more successful in the international arena. Also, the manufactured crises themselves—the specters of overpopulation, famine, pollution, and ecological collapse—should begin evaporating over the next few years. The doomsday-socialist alliance will find itself out in the cold without any crises left to solve. To be sure, the left wing will attempt to manufacture new ones—threat of invasion from outer space, perhaps—but we would do well to prepare for such an eventuality in advance.

In the following sections we will look at the doomsday projections one by one. We will see why most of them are either fanciful illusions to begin with, or else nothing more than temporary problems which the human race is on the threshold of overcoming.

III

Malthus Resurrected

1

Overpopulation. Famines. Energy shortages. Worldwide pollution and ecological collapse. According to the Doomsday Brigade, overpopulation is the root cause of most of the ecological crises we face today. Too many people means not enough food to go around; hence, famines beginning in the undeveloped countries and later spreading across the globe. Too many people also means eventual depletion of our natural resources leading to mammoth energy shortages in the near future. Too many people translates into more and more pollutants spewed into the environment, rendering our air unfit to breathe, our lakes and rivers unsuitable for swimming and bathing, our entire water supply eventually undrinkable. Overpopulation, goes the argument, will result in the final collapse of civilized society sooner or later—probably sooner.

"Is there hope for mankind?" asks the Doomsday Brigade. The answers range from a cautious *maybe* to an emphatic *no*. No hope for mankind. Humanity is doomed.

Columnist William Safire writes about "The Catastrophists," a hardy band predicting that the "population explosion will turn prairies into urban slums." Robert Heilbroner, in his book, *An Inquiry Into the Human Prospect,* warns us that overpopulation will lead to iron governments in developing nations resulting, ultimately, in nuclear war. "The freedom of man," he continues, "must be sacrificed on the altar of the survival of mankind."

"Is it possible to meet the challenges of the future without the payment of a fearful price?", Heilbroner asks. The answer must be "no, there is no such hope."

The Club of Rome, the official headquarters of the Doomsday Internationale, predicts total worldwide collapse sometime around the year 2020. Leading thinkers affiliated with this organization, including Italian economist Aurelio Peccei, Japanese systems analyst Yoicha Kaya, British scientist Alexander King, and American computer expert Dennis Meadows, fed all sorts of data into a computer and, to nobody's surprise, the computer arrived at an ominous prediction: all projections end in collapse. There is only one escape from oblivion, said the computer. Starting in 1975, population must be stabilized across the earth by equalizing the birth and death rates, and a series of "fundamental shifts in behavioral patterns must take place." People have to be programmed away from a lifestyle rooted in material consumption toward one of placid nonaggression. If this sounds as though the Club of Rome is suggesting a world federation, with B. F. Skinner appointed for life as Lord High Priest of Psycho-genetic Affairs, you're not too far off course.

The report issued by the Club of Rome may sound a

trifle pessimistic, but it is actually quite moderate compared to the "Blueprint for Survival" drawn up by thirty-three leading scientists in the United Kingdom, including the undauntable biologist Sir Julian Huxley, geneticist C. H. Waddington, and naturalist Peter Scott. "Population expansion," these gentlemen warn us, must lead to "the breakdown of society and of the life support systems on this planet—possibly by the end of this century and certainly within the lifetime of our children." It is not enough merely to arrest population immediately, according to "Blueprint." England must begin *reducing* its population by twenty-five million and return to an eighteenth-century agricultural society. In other words we have to jettison the entire industrial revolution and go back to the plow, back to sixteen hours a day of back-breaking labor on the soil, growing our own fruits and vegetables and cooking them in wrought-iron pots over open fires. These scientists, unfortunately, did not tell us *how* England was to reduce its population by twenty-five million people. Humanists right through to their Fruit o' the Looms, they decided to spare us the gory details. Better to leave these kind of unpleasantries to the imagination.

2

There is nothing really new about the current population explosion movement. It is the old Malthusian formula revved up to a higher level of hysteria, and coated with a scientistic veneer which gives it an appearance of respectability. Back in 1798 the Reverend Thomas Malthus presented to the world his famous dictum: population growth increases geometrically while growth in food production increases arithmetically. If this is true, it follows that any steady increase in population anywhere on earth is bound to result in dwindling food supplies, hunger, and eventual starvation.

It is somewhat incredible that the Malthusian Absolute is still taken seriously when it was at least partially discredited in Malthus' own lifetime. Contemporary Malthusians fail to inform us that their mentor qualified his formula in 1817, when he admitted that some population growth can be beneficial until such a time as a "proper or natural limit" is reached. During Malthus' final years his native country, England, was multiplying its population fivefold through immigration, rising birthrate, and declining infant mortality rate, while, simultaneously, enjoying a period of economic growth and prosperity. The same story was unfolding in the United States, which was increasing its population tenfold. America and England were becoming exporters of food and other products while importing labor from Europe. In the 1960s Hong Kong underwent one of the fastest population explosions on earth (largely due to mass emigration from Communist China during the Cultural Revolution), and became a bustling center of trade in the Orient. On the other hand, Ireland and Sicily; which have been losing people steadily since the beginning of the century, are among the poorest countries in the West. This may not prove that declining population is bad for the economy, but neither does it follow that rising population leads to shortages.

These facts hold no interest for the Doomsday Brigade, however. In 1950 Julian Huxley warned the world that there would be three billion people on earth by 2000 A.D., more than this tiny planet could possibly support. His figures were slightly awry, since we reached three billion in the 1960s without a worldwide collapse. Indeed, the overall living standard continues to rise each year, notwithstanding temporary setbacks here and there due to wars, poor weather, bad politics, and other nonecological conditions. Latest estimates for the year 2000 are in the range of seven billion people scattered across the globe.

The award for Noisiest Population Alarmist in America goes, hands down, to Paul Ehrlich. In *The Population Bomb,* Ehrlich throws out statements designed to titillate the fancies of necrophiles the world over. If the human race keeps procreating at its present rate, says Ehrlich, there will be only one square yard for every person by 2500. Why he stopped with that year is a mystery. It would have been much more effective to talk about people tiered on one another's heads in the year 2600. According to Ehrlich, we are increasing our numbers by one million a week, and not only are "hundreds of millions of people going to starve to death in spite of any crash foreign aid programs," but nothing now can "prevent a substantial increase in the world deathrate. . . ." From here he goes on to tell us that seven billion people will inhabit our little ball by 2000 A.D., and then he leapfrogs all the way to the year 2800 to paint us a scenario where the population of earth will be housed in a *two-thousand story apartment house which covers the entire planet*. Simultaneously, Ehrlich is predicting the total *demise* of humankind *and* a global skyscraper reaching to the stratosphere to house our overwhelming numbers. No matter which scenario transpires, you see, Ehrlich is determined to go down in history as a gifted visionary. Heads I win, tails you lose. Nothing wrong with that if you get away with it.

3

Scenarios everywhere. The Doomsday Brigade is fond of scenarios, the gloomier the better. Paul Ehrlich's, as we have seen, cover the Draconian gamut. What are his recommendations for bailing ourselves out of this procreational mess we have created? Among them are: prohibitive taxes on cribs, diapers, toys, and other baby items; reverse progressive taxation rising for each birth; government-authorized vasectomies; nationalized adoption agencies; and, *piece de resistance*, a powerful federal agency with the authority to take *whatever steps are necessary* to establish a "reasonable population level" in the United States. He declines to mention who should head up this agency. The only thing he leaves out is Jonathan Swift's Modest Proposal that we eat unwanted children. He suggests that we lower the population of earth to one or two billions of human beings.

Compared with Dr. Ehrlich, Philip Appleman is a veritable Pollyanna. In *The Silent Explosion* he claims that the projected world population of seven billion for the year 2000 is more than we can adequately feed, but he at least refrains from predicting the certain demise of civilization by that time. He sees some hope in the fact that Communist ideology, which long defined socialism as an economic system capable of providing abundance for everyone, is undergoing subtle changes. Both the Russians and Chinese are coming to grips with hard facts, and pure ideology is beginning to lose out to practical considerations. The traditional party line that "there is no such thing as overpopulation in a Communist society" is no longer being bruited about publicly. But this is as far as Appleman will go in the direction of optimism. His basic thrust is a modified version of Ehrlich's—more people means eventual disaster—and he favors political remedies to lower the birthrate starting immediately.

The Doomsday Brigade has lost little time in recruiting some of America's leading leftists to the cause. Our old friend, Max Lerner, will never be accused of modifying his ideology to keep pace with newly discovered facts. "The population problem is no longer a matter of option by the individual mother or the individual family," he states. "It has become a matter of national, even global, necessity." But of course. A Global Federation of Socialist States to handle the matter, no doubt.

Paul Kurtz, editor of the *Humanist*, regards "Blueprint for Survival" as a divinely-inspired writ handed down to mankind for our own good. If "Blueprint" says England must reduce its population by nearly half, then by all means let us get on with the job ahead. In his own proposals for the future, Kurtz is refreshingly open about his own racist attitudes on the subject of population control.

"Another pressing moral issue that we shall no doubt have to face is not only how to control the *quantity* of life—the number of human beings born and kept alive—but how to determine the *quality* of life, the kind of living creatures that shall be brought into being." After setting us up with this startling broadside, Kurtz goes on to call for worldwide eugenic planning. "We are rapidly approaching the time when not everyone who chooses can be permitted to bear and raise children." Repeatedly, his rhetoric is filled with phrases such as "nourishing the best qualities of human life." Then he hits us with his clincher, the point he has been building toward all along: "It is often the poor and underdeveloped in intelligence and capacity who tend to have large families. This means that a gradual lowering of the quality of the genetic stock is likely to occur without conscious eugenic planning aimed toward improvement."

Why stop with the lower orders? What about those whose *ideas* may be considered detrimental to the "common good"? Shouldn't they be eliminated as well?

In case after case, the social democrats spout the rhetoric of Nazism—a new kind of left-wing or *global* socialist Nazism. Paul Kurtz does not even bother to disguise it with the usual humanistic jargon liberals have made famous over the years. As a matter of fact, he has the unmitigated *chutzpah* to defend his totalitarian position with *libertarian* rhetoric. "I would argue for the libertarian policy concerning morality," Kurtz writes. "We may have to restrict the freedom of parenthood for the common good and for the freedom of others. I wish to argue that we are reaching a situation where the only way to preserve freedom may be limitation of population. . . . The demands of liberty require that we restrict the unlimited right of procreation. . . . If one is a libertarian, one would hope that the constraints would be kept at a minimum, consonant as far as possible with a maximum of individual freedom." As a final measure, which he hopes can be avoided, he advocates "mandatory sterilization of large numbers of the population, and required abortions imposed by court order. . . ."

Dictatorship for the sake of preserving individual freedom! If the liberals have any shame at all about their pregnant attempts to co-opt rival factions in society, they certainly have failed to demonstrate it so far. From Max Lerner's "Democratic socialism is the ultimate goal of Marxism" to Paul Kurtz's libertarian dictatorship: the liberal left has not changed its methods much over the decades. Its flanks, both left and right, must be shored up at all costs. They will not stop until they have drained our very language of every final drop of meaning.

4

The Doomsday Brigade. The Social Democrats. And the Anthropologists. All have enlisted under the banner of population control. From Max Lerner and Paul Kurtz we turn our eyes and ears toward Margaret Mead. There are several reasons why I dislike Ms. Mead, not least of which is the fact that she bears an uncanny resemblance to Eleanor Roosevelt—not quite so toothy perhaps, but an uncomfortably close facsimile just the same. Margaret Mead reminds us that "there is urgent need for battling the growth of world population," since "conservative estimates place world population at approximately seven billion by the year 2000." This figure has been repeated over and over again, with such urgency one begins to wonder if there is something mythically portentous about the number seven billion. Does a great adding machine in the sky click off numbers every day . . . 6,999,999,998 . . . 6,999,999,999 . . . 7,000,000,000 . . . with planet earth programmed for self-destruction as soon as it reaches that lofty figure? Save us all from magic numbers: 1984; 7,000,000,000.

Margaret Mead does not stop there, you can be sure. She proceeds to castigate (you guessed it) the Ugly Americans for using up 50 percent of the earth's natural resources while we constitute only 6 percent of the world's population. This is another favorite argument of the Doomsday Brigade. America consumes disproportionately to its numbers—42 percent of this, 57 percent of that, 46 percent of the other thing. This contingent, of course, fails to acknowledge that we also *produce* disproportionately to our numbers, that while we are "raping the earth" of all those beautiful natural resources, we are also converting them into commodities people can actually put to use. Never mind that, though. Let us all turn back to farming and let those natural resources lay dormant in the ground.

The feedback among these various groups—scientific, political, sociological—continues at a dazzling pace. Paul Ehrlich paints us a scenario, Lerner and Kurtz translate it into political terms, Margaret Mead feeds us the sociological implications, and Paul Ehrlich and Co. pick up the feedback and evolve the doomsday machine another step further along the road to world federation. Margaret Mead declares that Americans consume more than they ought to, and Paul Ehrlich comes right back with a new twist on the problem: "The birth of an American child is fifty times more of a disaster for the world than the birth of each Indian child." Why? Because we *consume* more, says Ehrlich. This puts him in the paradoxical position of advocating population control in the United States, where the birthrate has already fallen well below the Zero Population Growth level, instead of in India or Asia, where it still progresses at a hectic pace. Paul Ehrlich is not concerned about paradoxes, however. He seems to thrive on them. Facts don't matter. Nothing matters except his contradictory scenarios.

Author and movie-maker Susan Sontag does not limit her wrath merely to Americans, you will be happy to note. According to Sontag, "the white race is the cancer of human history." If we are going to control population, why not just reduce the number of white people infesting the world and solve all our problems?

5

The dark races are not so easily seduced by this type of rhetoric, however. Among blacks and Spanish-speaking Americans there is a growing fear that the population alarmists really mean to limit *their* numbers, notwithstanding all the talk of the cancerous influence of the white race. According to Nat Hentoff, minority groups in general seem to be against mandatory controls. Black political caucuses and Hispanic organizations are very much afraid that all talk of coercive controls is aimed primarily at them. They have heard too much from people like Paul Kurtz about the *quality* of life the government should permit to come into existence. Kurtz, unfortunately, is not the only one openly discussing the genetic consequences of an expanding population. He receives support from others like British scientist Sir Francis Crick, who foresees a day when "no newborn infant will be declared human unless it has passed certain tests regarding its genetic endowment. If it fails these tests, it forfeits its right to live."

How different is this attitude from the eugenic theories of Plato and Adolf Hitler? How far removed is the resurgence of a latter-day Nazism, a left-wing Nazism imposed over humanity on a global scale? Plato talked about separating the better stock from defective infants and putting them in "rearing pens" where they would be nurtured to maturity by the state. His putative Republic was at least limited to Greece. Hitler's racial mythology took on global proportions, and it has now been picked up by some of the leading proponents of mandatory population controls. The Doomsday Brigade. The Social Democrats. The World Federalists. A worldwide dictatorship with absolute control over every conceivable aspect of human activity.

Garrett Hardin, a colleague of Ehrlich's, is another one who is explicit about his totalitarian design: "A woman will be allowed to have X number of children, after which she will be required by law [World Federalist law?] to have an abortion and be sterilized." What would Freud make of that? Or Gloria Steinem, for that matter? Others of this ilk have talked seriously about "tattooing women who exceed their quota so the whole world can see their infamy." Yes, the feminist movement will be swallowed by its own ideology.

Sir Julian Huxley is equally blunt about his own political solutions. "If I am asked whether a country's and the world's population should be regulated, my answer is *Yes.*" Huxley seems to lament the fact that the human lifespan is increasing, and the infant mortality rate is declining in much of the world, since these apparent blessings are little more than the proverbial wolf in sheep's clothing. Procreation was fine "for centuries before," says Sir Julian, "while disease was cutting man down. It is so no longer, with our better conditions and more efficient medical achievements."

Ah, blessed disease! And cursed be the medical profession. All it is doing is prolonging human life.

Finally, Julian Huxley delivers his knockout punch—the sum and substance of his entire doomsday philosophy. Man, says Dr. Huxley, is "the cancer of the planet." Not Americans. Not the white race. But *man*. Man, you see, clutters up the globe and makes life unsafe for all the beautiful living things—like polar bears and crocodiles and boa constrictors. Obliterate him from the face of the earth and all will be serene again. Huxley wants the United Nations to establish an Agency for Population Control. Each nation would be forced to set up a commission to regulate its birthrate. "If once we manage to conquer this gravest danger of all, this senseless overproduction of men, we shall be able to conquer other dangers."

Yes, man. People. Humanity. The root of all evil. Destroy the race; shackle humanity to a totalitarian jackboot; turn mankind into an army of slaves; and watch the flowers bloom. And the weeds. And poison ivy. And make the planet safe for all the furry jungle creatures.

6

So the Doomsday Brigade has formulated the spaceship earth theory of existence: we are all travelers on a small imperiled vessel. Every vessel, particularly an endangered one, requires a captain. A leader. A Führer. Every imperiled vessel needs someone in command to tell others how to behave, how much to eat, how many children to produce. If we are all imperiled together, the actions of one affect everyone on board. Hasty, thoughtless, or selfish activity threatens the survival of the entire vessel. So many people have come to accept the spaceship earth analogy that it has taken on the proportions of a truism. Given such a premise, everything that follows is perfectly logical. If the earth is an imperiled spaceship, then the actions of each individual threaten the survival of all. We must all pull together for the common good. We need a world coordinator, a central planning board to ensure the safety of the spaceship.

Under careful scrutiny, however, the analogy does not hold up. The spaceship earth theory is based on a static view of the planet. *If* our food supply were a fixed quantity; *if* our energy sources were limited; *if* all the resources necessary for life support were static—then it would indeed follow that the earth is an imperiled vessel. Any increase in population at all would automatically mean a smaller slice of pie for everyone. But this theory overlooks the fact that man is a producer. We have it within our capacity to *increase* the food supply (which we have been doing all along) so that rationing is not required. Fairly soon we will no longer have to rely on the earth's natural resources for our energy supply, nor, eventually, will we even be confined to this particular "spaceship" for our *lebensraum*. Far from being an imperiled vessel, the earth is slowly being transformed into a garden of abundance, and a launching pad from which the human race will spread its wings further and colonize the rest of the solar system. "Spaceship earth" is nothing more than a clever analogy the Doomsday Brigade has concocted in order to terrify the citizenry into accepting its awesome political schemes. It will not work because its premise is a fraud. The doomsday-socialist alliance has erected a socio-environmental-political structure founded on quicksand.

So far as the population explosion scare itself is concerned, there are two basic ways of looking at it. First, is it true that mandatory controls are required to keep our numbers at a reasonable level? And, second, is it even *desirable* to limit our numbers? Something else we have all come to take for granted is that population must be limited either by voluntary or mandatory methods. But it is not at all clear that this course is the best one for mankind to take in the long run.

7

First: are mandatory controls necessary? The answer here is a decisive *no*! The history of industrialized nations has been one of a gradual leveling of their birthrates as machinery is brought onto the farms. With industrialization and mechanization of a country's agricultural industry, children have become less in demand as extra hands to work the farms. They become, instead, a drain on parents whose rising affluence is independent of manual labor. It makes far better sense, then, for population alarmists to support industrialization rather than oppose it as many of them have done with their asinine call for a "return to nature." Today the Western nations, as well as several Asian countries such as Japan and Taiwan, are totally industrialized. Mainland China, the emerging African nations, and much of South America are quickly following suit. There is even talk that the newer nations will skip the industrial revolution altogether and pass right into the new technological era. There is no reason to suspect that birthrates in these developing societies will not follow the pattern of the industrialized nations. Human nature is not limited to national boundaries. Peoples' needs and reactions to changing conditions are substantially the same throughout the world. Within the next decade or so we can expect to see a gradual slowing of the birthrate on a world scale, perhaps eventually a period of decline as in the United States, where it is now well below the Zero Population Growth level.

One of the countries most concerned about overpopulation is India. When India launched a *voluntary* vasectomy program in 1964 to control population growth, Paul Ehrlich stated (predictably) that it was destined to fail because of the reluctance of the citizenry and the technical problems involved in performing so many. Yet, by 1971 the turnout for voluntary vasectomies had so far exceeded expectation that the program was expanded to all of India's three hundred and twenty districts. No one is claiming yet that population growth is no longer a concern in India, but at least there has been a favorable response to a voluntary method of controlling population.

Another item the Doomsday Brigade never considers is the fact that two-thirds of this planet is covered by water, and the "square yard for every human" projections are invariably based on figures for land mass. We are now talking about building jetports at sea and, once this is done, the construction of hotels, shops, and permanent communities around the jetports will surely follow. In New York City there are plans for the development of a gigantic offshore complex that will include a jetport, nuclear power plant, waste-disposal center, and deep-water seaport. The technological problems have already been resolved. In Holland a variation of this concept has been realized in the form of Polders—areas reclaimed from the sea housing over seven million Hollanders.

Developers in Cleveland and Chicago have been studying proposals for floating jetports and other facilities on caissons in Lakes Erie and Michigan. Studies indicate that the sale of land-based airports to private developers could raise much of the money required for the projects. Eventually, the concept of floating cities further out to sea will become a reality. Environmentalists like to howl about the "desecration of the oceans" when these alternatives are suggested, yet they are the first ones to moan about "overcrowding" on land. Seaborne cities will solve the problem of living space for future populations (if it is a problem at all), and will also create thousands of miles of man-made "beach-front" which never existed before.

Amatai Etzioni, chairman of the Department of Sociology at Columbia University, makes the point that it is "impossible to control population" in the first place. We cannot even set up a target figure of, say, 2.1 or 1.6 births per family as a desirable goal since we do not have enough information at our disposal. Census figures in the United States are vague at best, and they are less reliable in other countries. We need far more information than we currently have and are *likely* to have, says Etzioni. The federal government admitted that it may have missed as many as a quarter of a million people in New York City alone—a city of eight million people in a country of over two hundred million. We don't really know exactly *how many* people live in the United States, let alone in the rest of the world. Attempts to impose mandatory population controls on the public are "like driving in the dark with very dim lights." "What we believe we know is often insufficiently documented." In the developing nations, all-out programs have had so little effect it is hard to measure.

Nat Hentoff is one democratic socialist who has come out against mandatory controls in this area. "Unlike B. F. Skinner, I not only believe in free will," says Hentoff, "but I also believe that a sufficiently informed citizenry will voluntarily choose to limit the number of its progeny." Hentoff's libertarianism, alas, does not extend to the economic sphere, as we have already seen. But at least he has not fallen into the doomsday trap with other social democrats and World Federalists.

8

Is it *desirable* to limit population growth in the first place? Nathan Glazer, sociologist and author, writes: "India, where there has been a concentration on curbing population growth, shows no marked success in moving out of abysmal poverty, or in achieving a lower rate of population growth. Other nations, such as Brazil and Mexico, where there have been no government programs of population control, have shown greater success in at least becoming prosperous." In the case of Brazil there has actually been a concerted effort to *expand* the population so that Brazil can become a major country by the 1980s.

The sheer number of people in China and India is usually blamed for their low standards of living. Yet, what the Doomsday Brigade never points out is that China, with its eight hundred million or so, has a population *density* of only two hundred per square mile—roughly a third that of England and a fifth that of Holland, which is importing labor from southern Europe to keep pace with a constantly rising living standard. Countries with the densest populations *and* relatively free political systems have been thriving in all areas—economic, social, and cultural. The concentration of people in limited areas, and a political climate permitting the free flow of their talents and energies, has generated prosperity and abundance throughout history.

As British agricultural economist Colin Clark puts it: "Even the case, that population growth causes inconvenience, cannot be substantiated. Far from being a disaster, population growth brings greater advantages—economic, political, and cultural—in the United States and in other countries. Proposals for the compulsory limitation of families, which would be an infringement of the rights of man in any case, are based on misinformation about the facts."

Clark goes on to strengthen his position with historical examples. He cites Greece in the sixth and fifth centuries B.C. as the first recorded incidence of rapid population growth on a limited land area. The result, according to Clark, was accomplishment in art, literature, science, and philosophy. More recently, "the world has acquired what freedom it has in the course of the last two or three centuries of rapid population growth, not in the long centuries of stationary or very slowly growing population that preceded them."

The same is true of economic freedom, says Clark. "Competition works better with a growing population [which may be a main reason why the socialist-doomsday crowd wants to limit population growth]." The line of reasoning here is, the more people there are, the higher the level of competition, and the more dynamic the resulting economy. Even Maynard Keynes, the economic guru of the liberal left, seemed to recognize this later in his life. Some of his earlier arguments for a controlled economy were based on what he thought was a fairly stabilized Western population in the 1920s. In 1937 he loosened up a bit and advocated a freer economy with more private decisions.

What the population alarmists really seem to be saying, when one analyzes their statistics carefully, is that our *cities* are overpopulated. UN studies indicate there are more open spaces today then there were a hundred years ago because of the exodus to urban centers. Then again, some social critics, most notably Edward Banfield in *The Unheavenly City,* deny that overcrowding is responsible for slum conditions in the central cities. Whatever the case, the economic conditions which gave birth to the rise of cities over the centuries have been changing since the end of the nineteenth century. There is no longer any reason for large numbers of people to cluster around employment areas. The exodus to the suburbs was made possible starting around 1880 with the advent of mass transportation. People can live farther and farther from their jobs and still commute in an hour's time. Now the jobs are following the middle class (working and middle class are virtually synonomous) into the suburbs, and there has been a corresponding spread of humanity beyond suburbia into exurbia.

(Paradoxically, the doomsday alarmists are urging the middle class *back* to the cities even as they lament the overcrowded conditions which presumably exist there already. One wonders how these people sleep at night with all these contradictory ideas crashing about in their heads.)

The entire pattern of population distribution is going through a radical change today—more broadly scattered with parks and green spaces in between. Those remaining in the central cities, to a large extent, are the comfortable and wealthy who choose to do so for aesthetic reasons, and the poor who have been lured from poverty-stricken rural areas with the promise of easy and eternal welfare checks. The horn of plenty is stuffed with an endless supply of taxpayers' dollars, available only for the asking, liberal politicians have been proclaiming for years. Soon, however, their cornucopian pipedream will be turning into a fading wraith. They will have to make good their promises out of their own pockets—or not at all.

9

The final question we have to face is: just how many people can the earth support in comfort? Here the estimates range from Paul Ehrlich's one or two billion (one out of two people currently alive has to go lest we all starve to death in the streets) to Buckminster Fuller's delightfully optimistic statement that there is *no outer limit.* Man, with his incredible ingenuity, can provide for everyone, says Fuller. More moderate spokesmen put the figure around forty or fifty billion, or roughly ten times our present three-and-a-half to four billion.

Who is right? Is there anyway to know for sure?

Two people on earth would probably be too many if those two were Paul Ehrlich and Buckminster Fuller. Ehrlich would be saying that Fuller had to be eliminated for the "common good," while Fuller would be trying to stick Ehrlich under one of his bubbles. It is difficult to take all of Fuller's schemes seriously, but in the face of the avalanche of pessimism we have all been subjected to in recent years, one is tempted to champion his gutsy proposals on principle alone. Fuller has earned the everlasting enmity of the Doomsday Brigade by claiming he could take the entire population of earth today and provide everyone with adequate housing and privacy on the islands of Japan. His plan calls for the erection of a mile-high apartment complex, with each unit containing its own power supply, garbage and water recycling systems. The structure would be designed in such a way that each apartment would be mobile and used for transportation over land and water.

Fuller manages to solve not only the population problem, but the housing shortage, the pollution, transportation, and parking problems as well.

Those inclined to shrug off this proposal with a laugh might do well to recall that Fuller's dymaxion houses and geodesic domes were once denounced as hopelessly utopian, and his theories on the tetrahedronal structure of matter, originally ignored, have made a profound impact in the field of subatomic physics. Fuller was talking about building homes with self-contained electricity and recycled water supplies in 1928, thirty years before this concept became a reality in American space capsules. According to Fuller, there is virtually no limit to the amount of people that can be comfortably supported on earth with proper architectural and recycling techniques. Whether or not one looks forward to sharing the planet with a trillion human beings tiered on top of one another, however comfortably, in cities reaching to the stars, we cannot help but admire a man with the courage to propose such daring schemes at a time when technology and procreation have become synonymous with "capitalist exploitation."

Another uncompromising optimist is Iranian-born novelist and essayist, F. M. Esfandiary. He has been called a "radical optimist" by *Publisher's Weekly,* and he considers pessimism to be based in a lack of historical perspective. He is not in the least concerned about expanding population, and he talks about floating cities in the oceans and the colonization of other planets as though these dreams had already been realized. "There is no way to fully anticipate the changes that will take place in the next twenty years, let alone the next hundred," says Esfandiary. "Changes are taking place so rapidly now, we might be living in a totally different world by 1990." He has no patience with those who want to return to a natural state. "These people go to Iran and they say, 'Look how quaint the people are in their ancient huts and native dresses.' Then they get back on an airplane and return to their airconditioned apartments and offices in the United States and Europe. There is nothing 'quaint' about living in ignorance and poverty, believe me. Technology makes everything possible—more people, abundance, unlimited affluence, everything. When I left Iran and came to the United States I skipped a dozen centuries. Now these doomsday alarmists want to roll back the clocks for everyone.

"They will not get away with it, though. Do you know why? They will not succeed because the rest of the world *wants* the freedoms and the luxuries of the Western world. It is only in the West that you hear this nonsense about turning back the clocks, and going back to the past. Poor people have had *enough* of the past. They are interested in the future. Let people like Paul Ehrlich live in Iran without their luxuries for a year, and you would soon have an end to their stupidities."

10

Between the extremes of Ehrlich and Fuller is Arthur McCormack, a Catholic priest who has written extensively on this subject. Father McCormack claims that a figure of fifty billion people seems to be the limit, considering the habitable land now available and the possibility that some of our desert and frost areas will eventually be cultivated. This number is based on land areas, and does not take into consideration the creation of ocean cities and colonization of other planets. At our current rate of population growth, we will have hit this lofty figure by 2110. But with the birthrate dropping in the United States and Europe, and expected to decline elsewhere on earth, most likely we will never come close to fifty billions of human beings.

Many population alarmists claim that the problem will be intensified by the drastic extension of the human lifespan, a development which seems to be poised just over the horizon. But, even if we learn to retard natural death from sickness and aging, the human race will still be exposed to the dangers of accidents and other forms of violent death. While we will surely succeed in lowering the deathrate within the next few generations—through major breakthroughs in anti-aging therapy, the control of cancer and the remaining killer diseases—this will most likely serve to reduce the overall birthrate even further for reasons which we will discuss in a later section. The type of reasoning which suggests that the obliteration of diseases and an increase in the productive life of the individual is to be feared rather than welcomed is the final extension of the doomsday philosophy to a *reductio ad absurdum.* It is Orwellian doublethink dressed up in a scientistic veneer. Sickness and death are good. Prolonged health and an extended life of vigor are evil. Good is bad and bad is good. Words no longer have any meaning to the Doomsday Brigade, and values are the opposite of what they seem to be.

Then again, what else can you expect from people who believe that, *not* only Americans, *not* only the white race, but humankind itself is "the cancer of the planet"?

IV

The Universal Breadline

1

Overpopulation and famine are usually discussed together, since Malthus established a symbiotic relationship between the two subjects. What he said, substantially, was that the pie cannot grow fast enough to keep abreast of the population increase. The slices available for everyone will inevitably become slimmer, until finally our individual portions are inadequate for proper nourishment. During the coming years hunger and malnutrition will spread from the poor nations to the affluent countries, resulting in mass starvation and worldwide famine.

At the United Nations in 1974, Secretary-General Kurt Waldheim warned the delegates that "stark, pervasive poverty afflicts two-thirds of the world, while never in recent decades have world food reserves been so frighteningly low." The spread of famine across the globe is discussed as though it were all but inevitable. Famine and political upheaval. Food shortages, say the pessimists, will generate massive political explosions. The burden of responsibility for this doomsday specter is invariably put squarely on the shoulders of the selfish Americans. A spokesman for the U.S. Food for Peace Program states baldly: ". . . even if it means becoming accustomed to such things as hamburgers made entirely of soybeans, Americans once again must face the need to share their riches, especially their food. Because, if we don't, we are likely to pay the price in political upheavals and stability in much of the world."

Ah, fascist Amerika! If our collective conscience will not spur us to fulfill our social obligations to the rest of humanity, why not try a little blackmail? Either feed the world voluntarily, or suffer the consequences of world revolution. Let's make our choice now.

"How many people will starve this year?" asks an editorialist in the World Federalist newsletter. Before you can mull the question over in your mind for an instant, the answer is blurted out with gloomy finality: fifty million people will surely starve to death by the fall of 1974; the figure could easily go as high as a billion. Fancy that. Nearly a third of the earth's population. If the scenario fails to transpire (as it did), don't you worry. Figures can be updated, and always are with dreary repetition. *Two* billion will fade into extinction by 1975. Or *three* billion by Easter of 1976. Sooner or later the Doomsday Brigade will be proved right—even if it has to put the torch to the next American wheat harvest. James P. Grant, president of the Overseas Development Council, is quite confident that rising costs "coupled with serious food shortages and increasing population make famine nearly inevitable for great parts of Africa, Asia, and Latin America." The mere transfusion of astronomical amounts of money to these areas will not stave off the coming disaster. What will? you'd like to know.

"Only an acceptance by the wealthy," says Mr. Grant without the slightest hint of a smile on his face, "of an unavoidable shortage of filet mignon, gasoline for Sunday drives, and Saran Wrap. . . . We and our industrialized compatriots of the First and Second Worlds must accept and further a lessening of our wealth and standards . . . not simply that the Third World might industrialize also, but so that the Fourth World—the earth's least developed peoples—might merely stay alive."

The Other America. The Third World. The Fourth World. Who, pray tell, will speak out for the Fifth and Sixth Worlds? Are they to be exploited eternally with no one dashing off to their rescue?

2

But Malthus has been discredited repeatedly throughout the years, you say. Never mind. Robert W. Dietsch, writing in the *New Republic,* is willing to concede the point. "For 176 years Malthus was wrong," says he. "Now his ideas are being resurrected. Populations have not been checked by any preventive means (war and birth control, as examples) and continue to multiply faster than food supplies, so the prospect is for peoples to be checked by catastrophic means—by famine." He quotes Addeke H. Boerma, director-general of the United Nations Food and Agricultural Organization (FAO), to the effect that "a turning point has been reached in world agriculture which bodes ill for millions more of the poor." New factors have come into play. Among them: world food reserves are at the lowest level since records have been kept; most of the world's arable land is already being farmed, and there is little hope of cultivating new land; worldwide food prices are soaring; affluent people (particularly Americans) consume too much of the world's protein supplies; and many others of a similar nature which we will look at more closely later on in this section.

This type of reasoning is frustrating. How do you debate with people who *admit* their mentor's ideas have been *wrong* for a hundred and seventy-six years—but are of cataclysmic importance anyway? One could easily collapse in despair, if there were not so much at stake.

James P. Sterba, a reporter for the *New York Times,* is not one to be outdone by his fellow ideologue on the *New Republic.* "The Green Revolution, launched seven years ago with great hope for vanquishing hunger, is sputtering along as little more than a minor revolt as Asia, overpopulated and undernourished, continues the struggle to feed itself," he writes. "The joy that accompanied the development of miracle rice and wheat seed in the mid-nineteen sixties has been tempered by skepticism and disillusionment as famine continues to stalk poor regions." According to Sterba, the gains in food productivity in underdeveloped countries over two decades—including the recent Green Revolution—have been wiped out by population growth. He claims that the spread of high yield plants has failed to have a significant impact on food production in Asia, and he questions whether the Green Revolution really exists in fact. "Those farmers who switched to high-yield varieties have often found that output has not increased much if at all . . .," writes Sterba, and he goes on to make the point that new agricultural technology in countries like India has only served to broaden the gap between rich and poor.

At least Sterba is giving us something to sink our teeth into. The mind boggles in the face of the general run of doomsday predictions—upwards of hundreds of millions or a billion people collapsing from utter starvation—without any significant facts to substantiate them. Sterba, however, is talking about specifics and we can thank him for giving us something tangible to gnaw on. It is possible to engage someone in dialogue if he is dealing in concrete examples instead of phantasmagoric illusions. When Henry R. Labouisse, the executive director of UNICEF, warned the world that four hundred to five hundred million children were going to starve to death in 1974 unless he had a hundred and thirty-eight million dollars to feed them, his figures had no meaning since they fell into the realm of Rabelaisian hyperbole. But when James P. Sterba makes the statement that "charts plotting production since World War II offer little evidence that a Green Revolution exists" in Asia, he is throwing out a specific which will either stand or fall on its own when all the available statistics are analyzed.

It is the old story updated for a new situation. The death of one human being is tragic since it can be understood; the death of a billion human beings carries with it the suggestion of science fiction. One can only stand back and observe the specter helplessly. The Doomsday Brigade, alas, is determined to destroy whatever merits its case may have with ideological overkill.

3

The failure of their projections to materialize on time does not deter the doomsday alarmists from their self-appointed task. In 1967 the brothers Paddock, Paul and William, published a highly-acclaimed book called *Famine—1975* in which they predicted that India would be ravaged by large-scale famines. These would occur possibly as early as 1970 or 1971, definitely by 1972 or 1973, and most of India's population would be decimated by 1975. The Paddocks promoted a "triage" system to save the world, a system used in military hospitals during wartime whereby only those patients with some chance of survival are given medical treatment. They advocated that the United States, as the most productive country on earth, initiate massive foreign aid programs to those starving nations with a small chance of survival, and cut out foreign aid altogether to less developed nations like

India which were already beyond hope. Fortunately for India, several private foundations ignored the advice of the Paddocks, and as a result India was able to develop a hardier wheat strain leading to a bumper crop in 1970.

India suffered a major setback in the early 1970s, due primarily to the war with Pakistan and Indira Gandhi's socialistic political measures, but India has come close to becoming a wheat-exporting nation on several occasions. Ms. Gandhi saw fit to nationalize her country's food shops and wheat production centers just when India was on the verge of achieving a substantial breakthrough, and food production declined drastically during the next two years. In early 1974, however, there was a move to return to a quasi-private market in both food production and distribution and, barring any unforeseen catastrophes such as earthquakes or war, India could become self-sufficient in food well before the end of the decade.

The Paddocks have made other ominous predictions over the years, among them: experimentation with rice and wheat strains would end in failure, and Pakistan would be wasted by famine before 1972. Statistics show that the development of hybrid rice and wheat enabled Pakistan to talk about exporting food in 1971, prior to the resurgence of its political disputes with East Pakistan and India. The Paddocks also condemned the Far East to certain annihilation, yet United Nations figures indicate that food production has been keeping ahead of population growth in this region as well.

Paul Ehrlich has of course presented the world with scenarios for every conceivable doomsday projection, including famine. In 1969 he informed us that it was utopian to expect underwater agriculture to increase food production in the near future. Farming of the sea is "another myth promoted by the ignorant or the irresponsible," according to Dr. Ehrlich. Yet, the facts show that advances in marine agriculture had played a decisive role in increased food production throughout Asia by as early as 1970—a year after Ehrlich's dire pronouncement.

Another bogeyman theory of the Doomsday Brigade is the "spreading desert" concept. Poor cultivation methods of the past have been turning much of the earth into desert, the theory goes, with 17 percent of it now arid and another sizable chunk too frost-covered to farm. This theory holds that poor farming techniques still being employed will increase this figure in the future. But here again we learn from UN statistics that most increases in food production during the past thirty years have been accomplished on land already under cultivation; in the United States, for instance, 75 percent *more* corn is being grown on 27 percent *less* land than was used in 1938. A new variety of rice developed in Taiwan has six or seven times the yield of the old kind, and is more resistant to adverse weather conditions. And if we should ever need additional farm land in the future, Arthur McCormack tells us that our arable land can easily be doubled with present methods, and multiplied eightfold with enough money and the newly developing technology.

Scenarios involving insecticides also received a good deal of publicity at the start of the 1970s. While concern that pesticides may eventually find their way into human bodies is justified, the alarmists have overlooked the fact that over thirty-five million tons of food—enough to feed more than five hundred million people—are destroyed by rats and insects each year. What can one say about people who claim to be concerned about inadequate food production in one breath, then turn around and demand the abolition of pesticide use in the next?

Irresponsibility, like benevolence and beauty, is something else which is in the eye of the beholder.

And what of those who shiver over the shortage of protein, and then denounce an American firm for attempting to export a low-cost protein supplement made from ground fish? They lobbied until the United States government banned the product from the market on the grounds that it was "unsuitable for human consumption." Presumably, the authorities with their boundless humanitarianism would rather see the starving masses provided with a pound of filet mignon three times a week instead. Sadly, however, there is precious little protein content in the good intentions of "humane" politicians.

4

Remedies to deal with the crises. The Doomsday Brigade is never short on remedies. There is only one remedy for the prospect of worldwide famine and ecological collapse, says Luther Evans. A world federal government must be created "with powers adequate to establish and maintain laws and justice on a world level. . . . We seek to convince the peoples and governments of the world that such a world federal authority is necessary for human progress, and that it is even essential to man's very survival."

World order and survival can be secured, says Evans, only by granting the United Nations enough power to pass laws which supercede the laws of individual countries; enough authority to govern the seas and outer space and administer the undiscovered natural resources of the oceans; enough power to raise adequate revenues through worldwide taxing power; enough power to enforce world law with a world federalist police force; enough authority to try all individuals and nations accused of violating world laws governing disarmament; and enough power to prevent any individual country (or person) from seceding or excluding itself from membership. In other words, the World Federalists want to make membership in their system obligatory. No country, group, or individual would be permitted to retain the arms necessary for defense in the event the world government grew a trifle too *pushy*.

This is certainly a reasonable remedy when you consider that the only alternative is the starvation of a billion human beings. Complete submission to a world planning board so it can destroy the freedom and prosperity of the United States and other industrialized cultures; so it can wipe out the benefits of a relatively free society and spread the wealth among the masses of the earth; so it can punish selfish Americans for consuming too much protein while other societies are undernourished; so it can turn the whole bloody planet into a socialist slave camp with *no* door left open for escape—unless, of course, one can erect his own spaceship and zoom off into the heavens.

A reasonable remedy, yes, except for two basic factors. Number one, it is impossible to level any group of people, no matter how small or large, in any direction except *downward*; and, number two, it would be sheer suicide for any self-respecting individual or productive society to submit to such a proposal without fighting with every last ounce of energy. No doomsday scenario capable of being devised by a human brain can justify such a Draconian political measure. It would mean, inevitably, the utter destruction of individual liberty, the end of all incentive to produce and generate a dynamic social and economic life, and the final collapse of civilization in every city, every village, every mudhole on the planet. It would mean that George Orwell's vision of 1984 had finally been realized, and the grim shadow of slavery had fallen over the earth. There would be no options left for humanity, no alternate societies to flee to if things got unbearable in one's homeland, no diversity, no variety, no eccentricity, no differences, no joy, no happiness, no spontaneity, anywhere on earth—nothing but a bleak desolate necropolis. The entire globe will have been transformed into a worldwide sanitorium for wasted and lifeless human beings.

This is why the Doomsday Brigade cannot succed, and why it will not succeed. This is why collectivism in every form must eventually be crushed, the sooner the better.

Its message is the message of death; its politics is the politics of destruction; its spirit is the spirit of despair; and its philosophy is the philosophy of hatred and human desolation.

5

And just how valid are the reasons for proposing such a remedy in the first place? What about these new factors which make Malthus' ideas worth resurrecting and reconsidering?

World food reserves are at the lowest level since records have been kept. According to the United Nations' own records, food production has outstripped population growth in the developing countries by 6 percent since 1952, and this figure is held down by countries such as Cuba, Algeria, China, Russia, Albania, and others which have nationalized, communized, or otherwise collectivized their agricultural industries. New technology, particularly in the fields of marine agriculture and computer farming, is expected to generate unprecedented crop yields in the near future. As we turn our attention more and more toward the oceans, we are beginning to understand that they contain a virtually unlimited supply of protein, in the form of ground fish and other marine life, for the human race. Another fact rarely considered is that India has nearly one-fourth of the world's cattle supply, but refuses to slaughter it for consumption because of rather quaint religious traditions. One-fourth of the world's beef, and India begs the world to save its masses from starvation. One is almost tempted to throw protocol to the winds and paraphrase Marie Antoinette: If they have no bread, let them eat meat.

Most of the world's arable land is already being farmed, and there is little hope of cultivating new land. Yet, as we mentioned earlier, the United States is growing more food on less land than it did in the late 1930s because of technological advances, and Arthur

McCormack, hardly a starry-eyed optimist, maintains that we can easily double the arable land on earth with present methods. The UN itself reveals that most increases in food production since World War II have been accomplished on land already under cultivation. According to Robert Katz, the author of *A Giant in the Earth*, the new technology will make it possible to feed virtually the entire planet from food grown in Kansas, and, looking ahead a bit further into the future, from food grown in the Sahara Desert. In 1974 the United States signed a peace pact with several Arab nations calling for, among other things, the cultivation of the Sahara for food production. Katz, whose book was written in 1972 and published in 1973, turns out to have been remarkably prescient in this regard. He makes the point in his book that periodic food shortages are *not* due to any deficiencies in technology or man's capability, but rather to bad political policies which restrict production, trade, and distribution. The problem, then, is not the lack of arable land, but the *proper use* of existing land and developing technology.

Worldwide food prices are soaring. Yes. So are the prices of double-knit suits, automobile repairs, books and newspapers, theater and movie tickets, surfboards, custom-designed slacks and shoes, yo-yos, railroad fares, and just about everything else you can name. The Doomsday Brigade is telling us, in effect, that inflation exists. Inflation has existed, in varying degrees, in many historical periods, and will continue to exist until we start developing sensible monetary policies. Prices are constantly going up everywhere, but in broad general terms our living standard has until recently kept ahead of monetary devaluation. This is an economic issue which bears little relationship to the ratio between food production and population growth.

Affluent people consume too much of the world's protein supply. Putting it another way, the famine alarmists are saying that *wealthy people overeat*. But, again, the wealthy and powerful have overeaten through the ages. The prevalence of gout in ancient Greece and Rome, and among the aristocracy of Europe, is testimony to humanity's inherent weakness for large quantities of spicy, delectable foods. Gluttony, drunkenness, promiscuity, sloth, and general dissipation are only several of the temptations man has succumbed to since the beginning of recorded history. Those with the wherewithal indulge themselves more frequently and elegantly than others. This is a given fact of human nature. One thing that has changed for the good, however, is the fact that today's wealthy, in the more mobile societies of the West, are usually the more productive people among us. In the past wealth and power were restricted to blood lines and other qualifications of elitist rule. In the freer political and economic climate of modern times, the poor have at least a fighting chance of rising out of poverty into the ranks of the "overeaters." Looking at the question another way, more sensible lifestyles seem to be altering our innate penchant for overconsumption, particularly as we learn more about the effects of poor diet and excess lard on aging and health. The Doomsday Brigade is basing this challenge on its *static* concept of the world: we have a fixed quantity of protein, and my overindulgence means less for everyone else. Hence, rationing is required. As we have seen, this simply isn't so. The pie gets bigger all the time, and food consumption is primarily a matter of personal taste —and psychological conditioning.

6

The Green Revolution. The most serious charge of all is James P. Sterba's claim that "the Green Revolution . . . is sputtering along as little more than a minor revolt," and gains in food productivity in underdeveloped countries over two decades "have been wiped out by population growth." This is a specific declaration about the human condition on a very real level. If Sterba can substantiate it, then perhaps Malthus is right after all. It would mean that the new technology has failed us, that all attempts in recent years to increase food production have not succeeded, and the specter of spreading famine is an ominous probability.

The Green Revolution was launched in 1966 in several Asian countries. The main goal, to put it simply, was the attainment of a higher crop yield on land already under cultivation. The first high-yield seed, called "miracle wheat," was developed at the International Maize and Wheat Improvement Center in El Batán Texococo, Mexico. The gentleman primarily responsible for the development of miracle wheat, Norman E. Borlaug, was awarded a Nobel Prize for his contribution. Next came the development of "miracle rice," this time at the International Rice Research Institute in Los Banos, the Philippines. The Green Revolution was off and running.

In the noncommunist countries of Asia, something like 10 percent of the rice acreage—amounting to twenty-five million acres—is planted annually with miracle rice. Both the Philippines and India were pioneers in adopting the new high-yield seeds. Miracle wheat has spread even more quickly, accounting for roughly 25 percent of Asia's wheat crop. The use of both miracle rice and wheat has grown steadily since the late 1960s, yet Sterba claims the Green Revolution is a failure.

How did he reach this conclusion?

He arrived at his pessimistic viewpoint after having interviewed several Asian leaders who told him that (a) many Asians did not like the taste of miracle rice at first because it was too starchy, (b) food production has not increased as much as expected in some areas because of the unavailability of necessary technology, (c) progress has been slowed by unpredictable weather conditions including floods and droughts, and by plant diseases caused by the *curtailment of the use of pesticides*, (d) 75 percent of Asian land is poorly irrigated and is dependent on an adequate rain supply, (e) wealthy farmers who can afford to invest in fertilizer, insecticide, and irrigation have grown richer while less affluent farmers live a more marginal existence, (f) the peasants who traditionally worked the land are being turned into the employees and tenants of wealthy investors who are buying up the land as it increases in value. This is the substance of James Sterba's negative comments about the Green Revolution.

Under close scrutiny, however, the arguments listed above ought to provide us with hope rather than despair. It is no doubt true that the new rice is not quite so tasty as the old variety, but just as Americans have gritted their teeth and learned to accept the taste of hothouse tomatoes for the sake of mass production and lower prices, so the Asians will (and already are) learning to live with starchy rice for the sake of their own survival. Later on, as their economy begins to prosper, they will be offered the options of tastier but more expensive rice or the cheaper miracle kind, in the same way Americans can still bring home a garden-fresh tomato from the supermarket if they are willing and able to cough up a king's ransom for it. Alas, the Asians are not the only ones whose tastebuds have been sacrificed on the altar of mass production and abundance.

Again, the fact that food production has been slowed because of unavailable technology is also a reason for hope. For it is not the Green Revolution itself that has failed, but rather the slowness of the powers in command in permitting it to work on a broader scale. The technology is already in existence and will be made available, and this potential for survival is far more significant than a temporary delay in its implementation.

As far as plant disease is concerned, we have already seen how the Doomsday Brigade itself is primarily responsible here with its hysterical demands for the abolition of DDT and other insecticides in the late 1960s. It is almost as though the doomsayers are consciously working to turn their grim predictions into reality—one way or another. If humanity fails to act out their scenarios, they will see to it that the conditions necessary for a worldwide ecological collapse are brought into existence. The answer, then, is to stop listening to them and return to the use of insecticides with whatever restrictions are required to protect the public from harmful side effects—a step which is already being taken in the United States and elsewhere.

What of Sterba's challenge concerning unpredictable weather conditions? So far there is precious little the human race has learned to do about flooding, not only in Asia, but everywhere else as well. This is a problem we will all have to keep working on. Droughts, however, can be alleviated by irrigation which is related to the situation discussed earlier: availability of technology. More and more of the earth's arable land is being brought under irrigation. The process is expensive and time-consuming, but progress continues. The problem is a cause of concern, but not of cataclysmic self-defeating despair.

The most interesting of Sterba's observations are (e) and (f) above, which are also closely related. These are especially interesting because they are more in the nature of economic and social commentaries than they are critiques of the Green Revolution. The rich grow richer while the poor stay poor or advance at a slower rate. Sterba (and those he interviewed) are more upset by the economic inequality generated by the Green Revolution than with its alleged failures. This is nothing more than the "gap school" of socio-economics applied to the Asian situation. What has happened there, of course, is that technology has rather abruptly jolted the Asian countryside out of a primitive and feudalistic agricultural economy into the early stages of capitalism. The land itself, and the technology required to work the land efficiently, have suddenly acquired value. A profit-and-loss, supply-and-demand situation has been injected into an economic vacuum. Those with sufficient capital to purchase land and invest in the new technology will necessarily become landlords and employers—or, to use an even dirtier world, capitalists. Those without the capital will become workers and tenants and employees. This is the essential model of a developing free enterprise economy, and it is only a "problem" or a "social evil" for those who happen to view it as such. Sterba and the leaders he interviewed obviously do. Left wingers of all persuasions tend to wince at the mere mention of the word *inequality*. It is inherent in their nature to do so, but this type of criticism has nothing whatsoever to do with the Green Revolution and food production in Asia. It is a description of a developing socio-economic condition (one which I regard as particularly encouraging and in harmony with the natural order of things), and nothing more.

As such it is irrelevant (to use a word especially favored by the left) to the discussion at hand.

7

If the Green Revolution has been such an abysmal failure in Asia, one could logically assume that these countries are on the verge of abandoning it altogether and returning to the old methods. Yet, statistics show that the reverse is true; the use of both miracle seeds continues to expand each year. Randolph Barker and Don Winkelmann, agricultural economists connected with the rice and wheat research institutes, are optimistic that the miracle seeds will be improved and their use will spread even further. Robert F. Chandler, Jr., former director of the Los Banos Institute, maintains that the new seeds and the technology which brought them into existence have given Asia a great deal of hope. "New goals of yield and production have been revealed," he says. "Many now see that the tropics offer the planet's greatest untapped resource for feeding mankind."

S. D. Athwal, associate director of the institute, makes

the same point even more succinctly: "What we are saying is, either you apply the new technology or you starve."

And Sterba, himself, grudgingly admits very briefly in the course of his long gloomy analysis of the Green Revolution that "the revolutionary seeds, and the technology that goes with them, still hold the potential for radically improving the lives of hundreds of millions of impoverished Asians, but that potential remains substantially unrealized."

The potential is there but it remains unrealized. This is a different picture entirely than he paints in his major conclusion—the Green Revolution is little more than a minor revolt, and there is little evidence that it exists at all. This kind of convoluted reasoning is rather like proclaiming the failure of aerodynamic engineering because airplanes continue to crash; or the failure of electronic communication because some people use telephones to make obscene calls. If one is determined beforehand to be dissatisfied with everything short of Utopia, there can never be any escape from nagging and demoralizing pessimism. It is far more realistic to regard each improvement in the human condition, however slight, as evidence of man's ability to save himself from oblivion and create a more civilized world to live in.

Utopia, implying as it does a world without change or surprise (once you've achieved perfection there's no room for advancement), must be a very boring place, when you stop to think about it.

8

Finally: cloning. At the risk of sounding like a utopian myself, the cloning techniques now being developed primarily in England offer the greatest hope for a virtually unlimited food supply during the next ten or fifteen years. Briefly, cloning is a process in which a cell from one animal is implanted in a denucleated ovum (one with the genetic traits of the female removed) in order to produce an exact physical replica of the cell donor. Cloning has been done successfully on frogs in England, and experimentation is now underway on higher animals such as sheep and cattle.

Picture this, then: cell tissue is removed from prime cattle at food production centers throughout the world. Through cloning, an *unlimited* amount of identical "offspring" is created from the best available beef sources. The same methods are applied to poultry, pigs, sheep, fish, vegetables, and fruit. The human race need never experience another food shortage again. With abundant supplies, the price of food can be reduced to a level almost everyone can afford.

Will cloning eventually be used in food production? It is a pretty sure bet that, once a thing becomes technically possible, it will inevitably be accomplished. The only variable is time. Exactly when it will happen is impossible to say. The sooner the better.

Will the Doomsday Brigade be silenced once and for all time when cloning eliminates the threat of famine from its list of scenarios? Not even an irresponsible optimist like myself would go that far. Rest assured, the Paul Ehrlichs of the world will find something else to be gloomy about. Just to beat them to the punch, however, there is one truly ominous aspect of cloning, and that is the prospect of human cloning. Leading researchers in the field say that the technological difficulties of human cloning have almost been eliminated. This is not a very pleasant thing to think about. Look-alike people traipsing across the face of the earth. I do not think this will come to pass, though, for reasons which I have already gone into in an earlier book. Since this is irrelevant (that word again) to the subject of food production, I will not get into human cloning here. If you really want to read about it, look up Chapter 3 of *Here Comes Immortality*—another irresponsibly optimistic book.

V

A Mountain of Garbage

1

And then there was pollution. The specter of world-wide pollution comes in third on the Hit Parade of Disasters conjured by the Doomsday Brigade. The prophets have erected a syllogism which goes something like this: people make filth; the more people there are, the more filth there will be; therefore, we have to reduce our numbers to keep from wallowing in our own poisonous effluvia. Simple enough when you stop to think about it. We are choking to death on pollution now. Pretty soon we will be buried under a mountain of garbage. The air is heavy with soot and bilious gas; our rivers and lakes reek of sewage and noxious chemicals.

People like Barry Commoner, Paul Ehrlich again

(always among the first to hop aboard a doomsday wagon), Howard R. Lewis, John Perry, and other catastrophists of this school discovered pollution a decade or so ago. Shortly after making this discovery they did a little investigating to determine its cause, and what do you think they learned? They found out that the two basic causes of pollution are people and technology. Man, the cancer of the planet, was up to his dirty tricks again. He went ahead and invented something called the Industrial Revolution which turned the globe into a veritable pigsty; then, as if that were not bad enough, he further developed his new technology to a point where it was going to kill off a billion or a billion and a half people—mostly Third and Fourth World people who are not as cancerous as First and Second World people—by 1975 or 1980 or 1993 or . . . well, sooner or later, anyway. Since the Industrial Revolution and technology were created by capitalism, it became apparent that the pollution of the environment was actually a capitalist plot (dare one call it conspiracy?) to destroy the oppressed peoples of the world. The natives of New Guinea could scarcely go swimming anymore without getting their loincloths smeared with oilslick. Tropical paradises all over the planet were being turned into festering cesspools by greedy capitalists and their foul discharges. The solution was clear: capitalist technology had to be destroyed, and the entire earth declared a wildlife preserve.

Then something else happened in the late 1960s which altered the picture somewhat. An international team of scientists decided to measure environmental pollution a little more thoroughly, and they learned that the rivers and air in Russia, Poland, East Germany, and other Communist countries were just as dirty as those in the West. A few among this group dared to say that maybe pollution was not related to capitalist economic organization after all; maybe pollution was just a natural byproduct of industrialization no matter where it occurs—

the United States, England, Japan, Russia, or even China.

The leaders of the Communist countries, and many of their apologists in the United States, did not like this interpretation. Mao Tse-tung claimed that socialist pollution was different from capitalist pollution, and his remarks were printed very respectfully in the *New York Times* (at least the editorial writers did not giggle over them). Fancy that. Socialist pollution is good while capitalist is evil, and no one chuckled. Where was H. L. Mencken when we needed him more than ever? American ecologists and the campus crazies continued to toe the party line for as long as possible, but after a while it became apparent that no one could take them seriously any longer. Pollution is pollution, period. And nobody with any sense at all could consider abandoning the Industrial Revolution, abandoning our factories and automobiles and airplanes and air-conditioned homes to return to the natural environment. The dichotomy established by the Doomsday Brigade—nature *or* technology, take your pick—was too ludicrous on the face of it. The doomsday-socialist alliance would have to come up with something better than that if it was going to make any headway in this area.

At this time, the doomsday prophets seem to have let up a bit on the pollution issue in favor of overpopulation, famines, energy crises, and, moving up quickly from the rear, the computerization of information on individual citizens (which I happen to regard as liberating rather than enslaving, for reasons we will get into in section VII). We can expect the Doomsday Brigade to return to pollution in the near future, however, as their immediate pet issues begin to decline in importance. The pollution scare has merely been shoved onto a back burner for the moment, not shelved permanently. For this reason we would do well to prepare ourselves ahead of time. It is worth taking a look at the true nature of this specter and understanding it for exactly what it is: a temporary problem which came about as a natural byproduct of industrialization, rather than a cataclysmic disaster requiring the attention of a global dictator.

2

A definition: pollution, put simply, is the contamination of the earth with harmful ingredients—ingredients which find their way into the bodies of human beings and do them damage. Long before man stepped onto the planet, the earth was busy polluting itself with flying ash from volcanoes, pollens, spores, molds, yeasts, bacteria, swamp gas, smoke from natural fires, and assorted fungi. More likely than not, the first of our species suffered from hay fever, asthma, skin eruptions, sinus trouble, and bronchitis as a result of natural conditions alone. There was not even a Mrs. Portnoy around yet to blame some of these afflictions on. Notwithstanding the claims of modern ecologists, the earth *au naturel* has never been a very hospitable place to live on. Man took nature as he found it, with its unpredictable temperature ranges and temperature patterns, and tamed it here and there as best he could to ensure his survival. Otherwise he would never have made it to the twentieth century.

Man's discovery of fire most likely accounted for the first incidence of man-made pollution. The burning of wood, bones, dried excrement (still used today in some areas), animal carcasses, fat, and everything else inflammable emitted elements that were less than beneficial to inhale. But it was the discovery of charcoal which resulted in the first serious threat to health, since this was the first known fuel to give off a lethal gas, carbon monoxide, while burning.

Attempts by government to control pollution are not especially new. The earliest antipollution codes banned the burning of coal *while Parliament was in session*, which gives us a good idea of whose welfare politicians usually have in mind whenever they get together. This attitude has been handed down to the present crop of legislators as though it were a precious heirloom. From Queen Eleanor of England in 1257 to Charles II in 1661 to the United States Government in the eighteenth and nineteenth centuries, the burning of coal has been recognized as a potential hazard to human health, but government has shown itself to be singularly ineffective in dealing with the problem. The reality of the situation has been vivid enough, and no one will seriously deny that the earth would be a more pleasant place to live on with crystal-clear waters and country-sweet air. But in its usually clumsy fashion, the Doomsday Brigade has come along and distorted reality into grotesque proportions.

Among the more incredible claims the ecologists have made are the following: pollution has impaired reflex time resulting in a rising rate of automobile and airplane accidents; divorce is increasing because of personality changes due to lead deposits in the body; many tornadoes are caused by pollution whipped into rotating patterns by air current; rising medical costs for humans and domestic pets are a direct result of air pollution; earth's overall temperature is going up, which will cause the polar icecaps to melt and the sea level to rise, resulting in the inundation of our coastal cities (when you stop to think about it, this might be one way of eliminating the major centers of air pollution, causing the temperature to go down again, the polar caps to refreeze, the oceans to recede, etc.); subtle genetic changes are occurring in the human body that will affect the evolutionary development of our species; and similar notions more suitable for Rod Serling's "Twilight Zone" than for serious consideration. Together with the World Federalists and other collectivists, the doomsday prophets have exploited this issue to create an anti-industry, antitechnology, anticapitalist, back-to-nature, no-growth ideology which has nearly succeeded in burying the real problem in an avalanche of self-serving rhetoric.

The pollution catastrophists defend themselves against this charge by claiming it is necessary to browbeat people in order to awaken them to the genuine dangers involved. Yet, I think the net effect has been just the opposite. People are not so dense that they cannot understand a situation if it is explained directly and honestly. They will tune out, however, if they think they are being nagged. After a while the senses become numb and nothing registers anymore. This is what has happened here for the most part, and the Doomsday Brigade has done the ecology movement a disservice with its shrill hysteria. People would rather not think about a situation at all if they are going to be subjected to a steady tide of pessimistic babblings.

3

The measurable effects of pollution have been well recorded, particularly as regards the combustion of petroleum derivatives starting in the late nineteenth century. In 1873 a black cloud settled stubbornly over London, accounting for approximately eleven hundred and fifty deaths. Londoners fell again to manmade "fog" in 1880, 1882, 1891, and 1892. Glasgow registered a thousand deaths in 1909, and the word *smog* was coined to signify the fusion of smoke and fog that had become a recurrent phenomenon. Belgium hosted a lengthy visit by smog in 1911 and again in 1930. In 1948 smog claimed its first American victim: Donora, Pennsylvania, in the valley of the Monangahela River south of Pittsburgh. A *potpourri* of steel, wire, zinc, and sulfuric acid particles was trapped in a temperature inversion, killing twenty residents and confining nearly half the local population to sick beds. More recent disasters include the London epidemic of 1952; the northeast corner of the United States in 1953; another thousand deaths in London during an eighteen-hour seige in 1956; London again in 1962; a week-long attack on New York during the Thanksgiving holidays in 1967; and serious pollution alerts in the Los Angeles area continuing into the present.

An estimated 40 percent of airborne pollution is a grab-bag collection from a variety of sources: toxic dust from cement works, lumber camps, steel and metal works, and agricultural plants; smoke from burners, furnaces, and both private and municipal incinerators; chemical gas such as ammonia, phosphine, chlorine, hydrogen cyanide, and phosgene emanating skyward from industrial plants. The other 60 percent is composed of carbon monoxide, hydrogen carbons, and nitrogen oxides emitted into the atmosphere by spark ignition engines. The assortment of contaminants in the air is so complex that it is virtually impossible to measure their precise effect on the human body. Various pollutants react with natural air components, forming additional lethal gases. The interplay between nitric oxides and the heat of the sun is said to produce large quantities of ozone which, according to the Doomsday Brigade, can accelerate the aging process and damage brain tissue. (One can already see Paul Ehrlich's next doomsday scenario taking shape: the earth will be overpopulated by a race of prematurely-senile human idiots in 2100 A.D. Unless, of course, we all starve to death first. Remember where you read it first, Paul.)

The situation regarding our waterways is even worse. Our lakes and rivers have been used as depositories for raw sewage and poisonous chemicals for generations. We started off with the naive belief that rivers could absorb everything we threw into them and renew themselves continually. After a while this practice became a habit and we blinded ourselves to the consequences. It was easier that way. Why rock the boat unless it's absolutely necessary? Procrastination is an inherent weakness of human nature. There is nothing conspiratorial about it; this just happens to be the way things are.

Those living in large urban centers are more vulnerable to the effects of pollution, since a temperature inversion can literally "lock the air in place" as though it were trapped by a huge invisible dome. With a high concentration of poisons in the air this is no different, in effect, than closing the garage door with the engine running. Sooner or later a benevolent gust of wind usually comes along to sweep the air clean, but during a prolonged seige many people (particularly those with respiratory ailments) can find themselves in serious danger. Even those in rural areas are not totally immune. Strong winds blowing for a long period have transported the pollution from a major city as far as two hundred miles across the countryside. The farm country of southern New Jersey is periodically visited by dirty air blown down from the industrialized northern part of the state, while fishermen far out in the Pacific have reported being engulfed by acrid clouds of smog which could have come only from Los Angeles.

As we noted earlier, the United States is not the only country to have experienced serious pollution problems. Every industrialized society, regardless of political makeup, is going through it—the most notable example today being Japan, which advanced a century economically in the past three decades. Those nations which are only beginning to develop now will be facing similar problems of their own in the late 1970s and 1980s. This is one of the prices of civilization: loss of innocence; social change and readjustment; industrialization; and environmental pollution.

4

Industrialization. Pollution. Technology. Progress. This is the natural order of things. The only way we can have a clean environment *and* maintain our high standard of living simultaneously is by exploiting the technology which caused the problem in the first place. The technology which brought us machines and automobiles and airplanes and radios and rocket ships and dirty air and water can now produce a pollution-free environment. Only technology can do this. There can be no turning back of clocks, no returning to nature and a simple way of life. There can be no abandonment of the present and the future in favor of the plow, of primitivism, of ignorance, of cruel and inhuman labor, of provincialism, of sickness and misery, of dependency on the whim of brutalizing nature. There can be no looking back to the past. Those who will survive and prosper will be twenty-first century men and women; they will be those who understand the past is dead and buried; those who realize that industrialization and capitalism are the greatest things that have ever happened to the human race; those who accept the fact that the New Technological Revolution has already begun and nothing will stop it. All the rest are counter-revolutionaries. They are reactionaries. The Doomsday Brigade. The World Federalists. Socialists, fascists, collectivists of all stripes. They are standing in the way of human progress and they cannot survive. Industrialization. Competition. Technology. Capitalism. These are the revolutionary forces at work which will complete the job of civilizing planet earth.

The technology which created pollution is already an obsolete technology. The spark ignition engine currently used in almost every pleasure car, for example, is one of the dirtiest imaginable. While it is theoretically possible to have a clean spark ignition automobile by keeping the engine perfectly tuned, and by using high-grade fuel designed for each particular engine so it is completely burned in combustion, these measures are expensive and unreliable. This type of engine emits three types of contaminants: carbon monoxide, hydrogen carbons, and nitrogen oxides. Until recently it has been difficult to find a filter capable of treating all of them simultaneously. The devices used for trapping carbon monoxide were not effective on the other two pollutants, and vice versa.

What are the alternatives? The diesel engine, also a gas burner, gives off relatively little carbon monoxide and hydrogen carbons, and a filter has been manufactured which traps nitrogen oxides with almost perfect efficiency. The gas turbine engine emits no nitrogen oxides, and the filters devised for keeping the carbon compounds from getting into the air are equally successful. Poor acceleration and low fuel mileage provided by this engine are standing in the way of its mass production, but these inadequacies are not insurmountable; research is continuing. Then there is a modernized steam engine, developed by the E. I. duPont de Nemours Company, which is negotiating contracts with auto manufacturers in Detroit and Europe. According to Dr. Theodore Cairns, director of duPont's research department, problems of size and complexity have been overcome, and the external combustion of kerosene and diesel oil create relatively little pollution. DuPont is already said to be receiving competition in the field from other engineering firms.

The idea of electric automobiles has been kicking around for quite some time. The transformation of propane into electric energy is considered much more efficient than the combustion of gasoline, and it is clean. Reduced maintenance and energy costs would offset the extra expenditures for battery recharges. A major drawback here is that the problem of size has not yet been solved, but some engineers maintain that experimentation on golf carts, minibuses, postal vans, and other special vehicles is producing better results. Electric cars are also small and durable, an important consideration when you think of the parking situation and the shape of the economy.

In addition to all these, Ford has acquired the rights to manufacture the Stirling engine, which was actually invented more than a century and a half ago by Robert

Stirling, a Scottish reverend. This is an external-combustion machine capable of running on virtually any type of fuel. The Philips Company of Holland has been refining and simplifying it since the late 1930s, and it is now extremely clean, quiet, and economical on fuel. Ford plans to develop this engine over the next few years before going into mass production.

Mass transportation promises to be more efficient and cleaner in the future, as government stands aside and lets new developments in the private market take over. Our state-subsidized railroad system is both obsolete and wasteful. The federal government is pouring our tax dollars into nineteenth-century technology which has long ceased to function properly. This is like trying to inject life into a dead horse instead of giving it the burial it deserves. In the near future we will be riding on air-cushion and magnetic-levitation trains which are fast, quiet, and clean. Levitrains, riding on electric cushions slightly above the rails, are now operating in West Germany. When perfected, they will be able to transport people at speeds up to five hundred miles per hour. Tracked-Air-Cushion-Vehicles, carrying passengers around the country at a hundred and fifty miles an hour, are scheduled for the United States by the late 1970s. With this type of mass transit system in existence, the public may finally be enticed away from the automobile —at least as far as commuting back and forth to work is concerned. For the moment, however, the private car still remains the cheapest and most reliable means of transportation, and attacks on its use by public officials are both arrogant and laughable when you consider the alternative government is offering.

Another new concept in mass transportation may be offered by the Zisch-boat, invented by Dr. Felix Wankel, who also developed the Wankel-rotary engine named after him. This, along with the air-cushion boats already in existence, can eventually be used to carry commuters down the Hudson and East Rivers, across San Francisco Bay and other waterways to save time in the future.

Yes, the technology which brought us affluence and abundance as well as dirty rivers and air is now obsolete, and it is being replaced by a new technology, a clean and more efficient technology. It was the genius of the marketplace which generated the first Industrial Revolution—and its inevitable side-effects. And it is this same genius, the free flow of energy and talent not only in America but everywhere an element of capitalism is permitted to exist, which will eliminate the undesirable by-products of industrialization and launch the twenty-first century ahead of schedule.

5

The word *soot* is synonymous with *filth*, but actually soot is composed of over a hundred different elements, including more than twenty metallic compounds, scores of chemicals, and many organic solids. By reclaiming this soot before it is thrown off into the environment, industry can harness billions of dollars a year in reusable commercial products. Trapping devices are now available which collect these pollutants and recycle them back into production. Hydrogen sulfide is recycled into sulfur, and metal particles are reprocessed into salable products. Industry is quickly learning that it is profitable to recycle, and antipollution equipment is a good investment.

Examples of this include: a power company, which formerly paid to have fly ash carried to a dump where it was burned by municipal incinerators, now sells it to cinder block, cement, and paving companies; alfalfa dust which used to escape into the atmosphere is now trapped and sold as high-protein cattle feed to ranchers; chemicals, previously poured into rivers and lakes, are now collected and pumped back into production; electrostatic precipitators installed by utilities do a more thorough job of burning fuel and reducing harmful emissions; Japanese companies which have collected ordinary garbage are now selling it for landfill, and European and American firms have started reprocessing it into building materials; Shell Oil Company, which was accused of polluting the oyster beds in Puget Sound, cooled and purified its discharges to the extent where it is now cleaner than the sound's water itself; the list grows longer every day. Antipollution technology is now a major industry. Within the past few years new companies have been created with the sole purpose of manufacturing and installing pollution-trapping machinery for a rapidly expanding market. And the boom is only in its infancy.

Land developers are now building entire new communities, offering both the latest conveniences *and* a pristine environment. Disney World in Florida is virtually a private government with its own mass transit system, private housing, and antipollution codes. City planners and architects from all over the world have been making pilgrimages to the Disney communities to discover how the great visionary was able to put it all together while our public facilities are crumbling with decay. There are plans for residential Disneylands to be built throughout the country, and General Electric has constructed a model for an all-electric, pollution-free, privately-developed city of the future. Indeed, most of the major land developers in the United States and Europe have broadened their scope considerably during the past few years. They are no longer putting up mere housing developments. The trend is toward total communities, complete with man-made lakes, ski slopes, tennis courts, golf courses, shops, schools, transportation, and, of course, the latest pollution-free technology.

Levitt and Sons (of Levittown fame) has already developed a miniaturized sewage-treatment plant the size of a one-story house, for installation in future private communities. It is reportedly both odor- and noise-free, and discharges effluents clean enough to swim in. A conventional treatment plant of the same capacity requires a minimum of six acres. Levitt also plans to market his invention to various municipalities for use in different neighborhoods throughout our cities.

Another private company, Automata, Inc., is erecting "the world's most ecologically-minded waste disposal system" in an office building in Chicago. The so-called Garbage Monster, officially known as the System of Maceration and Transportation, will "chew" an incredible amount of paper and soft garbage every day, mix it with water, biocides, and disinfectants, and dry it all to the consistency of sawdust, which in turn will be remanufactured into paper towels, egg cartons, and other "paper" products. In addition, the Garbage Monster will compact tens of thousands of soda cans and other metal products every week, and this will be sold for an estimated sixteen dollars a ton—enough to cover the cost of the entire system. This is all being done by and for private industry, but it is easy to see that the same ingenuity in government could save the taxpayer a lot of money, as well as a lot of grief caused by the contamination of our beaches by garbage which government tosses in the oceans.

Other solutions to the pollution problem now being generated by private industry are: a system designed by Westinghouse for making simulated-wood furniture out of shredded newspaper; tough, odorless, and sanitary tiles made from pulverized glass and cow dung by the Glass Containers Manufacturers Institute; a plan devised by American Solid Waste Systems for transforming garbage into solid bales for land reclamation. A less-publicized form of pollution—noise pollution—is also being combatted by International Harvester, which has invented a noise-suppressing metal alloy for use in power tools, propellers, brake discs, and subway wheels. A compound of copper, manganese, and aluminum, the alloy suppresses noise in metals by inhibiting vibrations.

The technology required to clean up the environment is already in existence, and more is on the drawing boards. This technology is a natural outgrowth of the

Industrial Revolution. Its usage is inevitable for a very basic reason—the best reason of all: good ecology is a highly profitable business, and industry always moves in to fill an economic vacuum.

6

Even as we consider measures for fighting pollution, the fight is already being waged. It wasn't so long ago that the Doomsday Brigade was seriously calling for new factories to be built with mile-high smokestacks to carry pollution above our air supply. The problem of how all that heavy soot was going to make it to the top didn't bother the doomsday crowd. *That* was an *engineering* problem—along with keeping the soot from falling back to earth once we got it up there.

Another pet solution being bandied about in the late 1960s was the development of a gigantic underground exhaust pipe into which *all* the pollution of earth would be funneled. The major obstacle here was finding a place for it all to come out. But that, too, was just another engineering problem. Then there were those who suggested putting it in orbit around the sun—an extremely costly remedy, to say nothing about the aesthetics involved.

The big question remaining is, what do people do *now* to protect themselves against the harmful effects of pollution, while they are waiting for the new technology to solve the problem for them? Since government itself is a major source of pollution, can we realistically expect our elected officials to look after the best interests of the public? The problem is compounded by the fact that, to one extent or another, everyone is a polluter in an industrialized society. Do we want to create a situation where everyone who drives a spark ignition automobile, or burns leaves in his yard, or smokes a cigarette in public is subject to a fine or a jail term? A certain amount of trade-off is necessary if we are all going to live in peace with one another. Pollution becomes a matter of serious concern only when it crosses beyond the limits of ordinary trade-off—when it constitutes a threat to life, health, and property. Then it becomes an act of aggression which the public has a right to defend itself against.

The trouble with many of the pollution codes established by various levels of government is that they turn out to be largely ineffective, or else there is an element of corruption involved. In White Plains, New York, for example, the city fathers determined that apartment house incinerators could no longer be tolerated since they were spewing too much filth into the air. So they passed a city ordinance requiring all landlords to convert their incinerators into garbage compactors by January 1973 (if memory serves me well). No more incineration of garbage, no more air pollution. Right?

Wrong.

At an investment of approximately ten thousand dollars per building, which landlords had to absorb, they made the conversions. The garbage was then carted to the *city* incinerator where it was *decompacted* and *burned*; in effect, the city ordinance served merely to centralize the problem to one mammoth incinerator. The government of New York State then stepped in and put White Plains on notice that its municipal incinerator failed to meet the requirements of statewide pollution codes. White Plains was told to upgrade the city incinerator at a cost of over four million dollars—which, of course, would be covered by local taxpayers. A subsequent investigation revealed that one of the White Plains councilmen, who had been most instrumental in passing the ordinance, had a controlling interest in all the compactor companies serving Westchester County. The ordinance did not give the landlords the options of upgrading their own incinerators, recycling, or finding another means of complying with clean air standards. They had to install the compactors or face astronomical fines compounding with interest for every day they failed to do so. The net result: totally ineffective antipollution legislation, windfall profits for at least one crooked politician, higher taxes to upgrade the municipal incinerator, and a new obstacle against the construction of high-rise apartment buildings in an area where they are urgently needed.

All this in a city—an overgrown village really—of fifty thousand residents, relatively small as governing units go these days. Magnify this type of inefficiency and corruption to a level of eight million New York City residents, seventeen million Californians, and two hundred and five or six million Americans, and you get some idea of the problems involved in trying to control pollution through the executive and legislative branches of government.

The newest antidote to political corruption being pushed by the left is the concept of an ombudsman, originated in Scandinavia. Variations on this theme include the appointment of a consumer affairs advocate or public watchdog to see that the public interest is served. But, then again, who is going to keep an eye on the watchdog to make sure he or she doesn't get bought off? Whose interest can we expect a consumer affairs advocate to serve? The consumers' or the official who appointed him in the first place?

No, asking government to protect us against pollution is like asking Al Capone to mind the silverware when we go away for the weekend. He *may* not rob you blind while you're gone, but it's a risky gamble all the same.

7

The best solution for the private citizen is to take to the law courts whenever he thinks his rights have been violated. Within the past few years a number of organizations, and individual citizens in several cases, have brought suit against both corporations and various government agencies for polluting the environment. Awards have been granted whenever damage to health and/or property can be demonstrated. In 1970 Governor William G. Milliken of Michigan signed a bill allowing the public to file antipollution suits against public agencies and private corporations. Michigan became the first state specifically to open up the judicial system in this area, and it would be desirable for other states to follow suit. Whenever a dispute arises between two individuals or factions, arbitration is always the fairest method of resolving it.

To those who say this is not a perfect solution, we can only reply that there are no perfect solutions. Abandoning technology and making it impossible for industry to function is no solution at all. This is a perfect example of tossing out the baby with the bathwater. Technology is here to stay, and fairly soon we will have a much cleaner environment. We will have the best of both worlds simultaneously.

Meanwhile, there are only three basic means of resolving disputes: we can slug it out in the streets; one faction can bully the other through unfair, self-serving laws; or we can take our case to court and hope the judge is honest enough to render an impartial verdict. This is not Utopia but, as we mentioned earlier, Utopia would be a very boring place to live in.

VI

The Eternal Brownout

1

In 1972 two professors at C. W. Post College on Long Island, Lawrence Rocks and Richard P. Runyon, made a series of predictions: by 1975 the United States government would find it necessary to restrict heating and air conditioning in all public buildings, schools, homes, hospitals, and other institutions; by 1977 government would move in to control or nationalize our major industries to ration energy supplies; by 1980 the country would be saddled with severe gasoline rationing; 1985 would see a massive depression on the scale of 1929; 1987 would bring a world-wide conflict over energy sources, possibly leading to World War III; by 1990 the shortage of copper would be so severe as to bring our electrical conduction technology to a virtual collapse; the year 2000 would find the planet in the grip of an irreversible water shortage; by 2030 a rising world temperature would cause the polar icecaps to melt gradually, resulting in the death of the planet through flooding. During the course of this long doomsday scenario, civil liberties would be totally eroded in the United States and elsewhere. The First Amendment would be repealed, and critics of the government's energy policies would be jailed under new antisedition laws. The shadow of totalitarianism would fall over the entire globe.

By winter of 1973-4 it appeared to many Americans as though the above scenario was beginning to take form. Gas stations were closing down all over the United States, particularly in the Northeast, while prices were shooting up from a dime to twenty cents a gallon. Many states imposed some form of a rationing system on the citizenry, in most cases an alternate-day purchasing requirement according to the number of the license plate. Oil companies were castigated on the floor of the United States Senate by demagogues like Scoop Jackson, and executives were hauled in for questioning without the basic constitutional protections afforded to defendants in a rape trial. If there was one dominant message emanating from left-wing politicians and the liberal press at the time, it was this: these oil barons on the stand before you are the enemy. The television camera skewered them on an electronic poker, and held them up for public humiliation. They were not even given equal time for rebuttal.

Yes, the politicians needed a scapegoat—anyone would do so long as he served to divert public wrath from the hallowed ranks of government—and they found it in the oil industry.

New controls were inflicted on the economy (which was already half-dead under the weight of previous regulations), and legislation calling for everything from the outright nationalization of the oil companies to rigid price controls was proposed. Gasoline supplies were allocated to various regions of the country on a priority basis, and the public was told it had better prepare for a minimum of two and maybe five or more years of severe energy shortages. The days of cheap, abundant energy for Americans were over.

Our old pipe-tamping friend, Luther Evans, used the occasion to write a letter to the secretary-general of the United Nations. "Your Excellency," he began (for some reason he declined to address him as "My Worship" or "Mein Beliebter Führer"), "As the President of World Federalists in a country which utilizes a highly disproportionate share of the world's resources, I believe that our membership (15,000+) earnestly agrees that the situation confronting all countries should be examined by all their representatives. . . . None of us can accept the idea of leaving to each nation the responsibility of independently solving its energy and materials problems.

"Algeria's Ambassador Rahal synthesized the question extremely well when he asserted that oil prices and the energy crisis are but one element of a much wider problem—that of bringing about an equitable relationship between the wealthy nations and the poorer ones. . . . As President Ahmed Hassan Al-Bakr of Iraq has eloquently stated, 'the best framework for discussing [the question of energy and overall resources] is the United Nations Organization. The United Nations is the only legitimate body in the world on which devolves the responsibility for regulating international life in all its fields.' "

Now if that's not *humane*, I don't know what is. The man is obviously *concerned*—concerned about his own gluttonous country which consumes too much of the world's energy supplies, and concerned about those enlightened leaders of Algeria and Iraq who think the United Nations should distribute a little of America's wealth in their direction. He is so humane he thinks we need a global king to solve not only the energy crisis, but every international problem that arises. You can't help liking a man with so much kindness flooding through his veins.

2

In an attempt to add a semblance of balance to the anti-industry hysteria generated in congress, Frank N. Ikard, president of the American Petroleum Institute, wrote a letter of his own to the *New York Times* which was published on February 28, 1974. In it he exposed the federal government as the prime culprit in creating the energy shortage of late 1973 and early 1974. It was the government, said Ikard, which "prevented the construction of the trans-Alaska pipeline for six years" after approximately ten billion barrels of oil and twenty-six trillion cubic feet of natural gas had been discovered in Alaska's North Slope; delayed the leasing of outer continental shelf properties where a hundred and ninety billion barrels of oil and eleven hundred trillion cubic feet of natural gas could be mined; "placed a five-year moratorium on drilling in the Santa Barbara Channel" which contains about four billion barrels of potential crude oil reserves; controlled the price of natural gas below its free-market level for over twenty years and discouraged investment in this area; imposed five hundred million dollars in additional taxes on the oil and gas industries "just when the first signs of an approaching energy shortage were beginning to appear"; urged greater dependence on foreign oil "at a time when the government should have been encouraging the development of American reserves"; legislated unrealistic emission controls on new automobiles which automatically increased our gasoline consumption by "fifteen million gallons a day"; "adopted sulfur-emission regulations which went far beyond those needed to protect human health"; and delayed the construction of nuclear power plants throughout the United States.

To be sure, the oil industry was at least partially responsible for the crisis since it had effectively lobbied in favor of import quotas for quite some time, and attempted to establish an international cartel to drive the small independents out of business. But the basic thrust of Ikard's argument is right on target. In attributing blame for the fuel shortage that had gripped the entire world, the overwhelming burden of responsibility fell squarely on the shoulders of public officials. It was not as though the energy crisis had erupted overnight. The warning signs had been visible for several years. During the three previous summers, various sections of the United States had been subjected to periodic brownouts and reductions in electricity supplies ranging as high as 8 percent. Americans had grown used to the sight of dimming lights in their homes, television pictures suddenly shriveling up toward the center of their huge screens, and air conditioners fading down to a low hum instead of revving away at full blast. Utility companies, which had previously urged their customers to gobble up all the electricity they could, had suddenly changed the tune and were telling the public to "save a watt" whenever possible. In the winter preceding the great energy shortage of '73-4, schools had closed down in the Midwest and mountain states for lack of heating oil, and gasoline stations had already been experiencing scattered shortages as early as spring 1973.

Yet, our politicians closed their eyes to it all and continued the same myopic policies that were gradually bringing an entire nation to its knees.

In April 1973, Time, Inc., sponsored a three-day energy conference at Lyford Cay in Nassau, the Bahamas. In attendance were representatives from government, industry, environmental organizations, and research institutions. Spokesmen for several energy companies informed the assemblage that a severe energy shortage was, indeed, looming over the near horizon, and they suggested a series of policy changes to alleviate the situation: increased production of domestic oil and natural gas, and the construction of new power plants, refineries, and pipelines; elimination of price controls on natural gas, which were fixed below 34 cents per one thousand cubic feet while the market level had been as high as 56 cents; and the easing of environmental restrictions to permit drilling offshore and on federal land. These proposals were immediately attacked by the environmentalists. Thomas Kimball, head of the National Wildlife Federation, claimed that industry would reap "windfall profits" if price controls were lifted on natural gas. He argued for a "national energy policy" assuring the public of a pristine environment *and* abundant low-cost energy simultaneously—an Alice-in-Wonderland suggestion if there ever was one. All we needed was a fairy godmother with a magic wand to implement it. Presto: the lakes are filled with champagne and the air smells like strawberry aerosol spray. Chango: clean energy comes shooting down to earth like starshine from a magic generator in the sky.

S. David Freeman, director of a Ford Foundation research group, tried to conciliate the ecologists by claiming that hundreds of utilities, gas, coal, and oil companies were all competing for an advantage in the marketplace, and could never coordinate a "conspiracy to raise prices." In effect, he was giving them the old *laissez-faire* argument that competition generates both abundance and the lowest possible free market prices, rather than monopolies and conspiratorial cartels. But to no avail. Logic has very little impact on humanitarian instincts. The environmentalists want the best of all possible worlds, and they expect government to deliver it to them by pressing a magic button located somewhere inside the halls of congress. If they were seriously interested in protecting the environment from greedy exploiters, one should think they would welcome higher fuel prices. The net effect of costlier fuel would be to decrease demand and hasten the search for cleaner energy sources which ought to be more acceptable to the Doomsday Brigade. A Harvard University computer recently predicted that energy consumption would triple in the next twenty years if prices remained unchanged, whereas it would not even double if the cost went up 50 percent.

The ecologists, as usual, are arguing against their own best interests by attacking free market competition and demanding Utopia by government decree tomorrow morning.

3

President Nixon was induced to take some measures toward alleviating the situation in the dark twilight winter of 1973-4. He urged congress to drop price controls on new discoveries of natural gas, and to extend tax credits to spur energy production in the United States. "Self-sufficiency by the 1980s" became his war cry. He was, of course, subjected to a heavy barrage of criticism from the professional ecologists, and we all know what happened when pressure was applied to Richard Nixon before. Crippling wage-and-price controls were imposed on the economy by this supposedly free enterprise-loving president. According to Herbert Stein, Nixon's chief economic adviser at the time, the president never imagined for a moment that wage-and-price controls could work. "What else could he do, though, when the polls showed that 75 percent of the American people wanted them?"

What he could have done was forgotten campaign politics for a while and taken the unpopular route; he could have followed his own convictions instead of sacrificing them for a short-term political gain—one with long-lasting economic consequences over every conceivable aspect of the economy. In this case, however, the energy situation seems to be abating. The energy crisis which was supposed to last a minimum of two and maybe five or more years was over inside of six months, and, in the early summer of 1974, the newspapers were headlining a worldwide energy surplus because of increased production in the Middle East and elsewhere. While I am writing this there are gasoline price wars in various parts of the country (including the Northeast, which was most seriously affected six months earlier), and several major oil companies are talking about lowering prices further at the pumps. There is no guarantee that this situation will continue. It depends, largely, on government maintaining a hands-off policy on the issue. The energy shortage we have all been hearing so much about was never due to a real shortage of natural resources.

Our own reserves of oil and natural gas are sufficient to last at least until the end of this century, while foreign supplies can satisfy the energy needs of the entire world until the middle of the twenty-first century. The problem was manufactured primarily in the political arena.

4

And now a whole new technology is being developed which will, eventually, free us of our dependence on these limited resources. As late as 1972 the experts were saying we could not have solar energy before the year 2000, while fusion power would remain a technological impossibility until the latter half of the next century. By that time, the human race will have depleted all the available energy supplies, and the planet will enter a new Dark Age—a period of never-ending night.

Most of us accepted these projections for solar and fusion energy on face value. After all, if it was technologically unfeasible to have them earlier, there was precious little anyone could do about it. Then, lo and behold, in the midst of our great energy crises the newspapers were running stories about commercial buildings *already under construction* which would be at least partially heated by the energy of the sun, and homes with solar heating and cooling systems which would be available on the market by the end of 1974.

Twenty-six years ahead of schedule!

In April and May 1974, articles were appearing in our major newspapers about "significant new breakthroughs" in the field of nuclear fusion. The scenario had suddenly been altered from no fusion power at all before 2050 to fusion plants operating in the United States in the 1980s.

Seventy years ahead of schedule!

What happened to change the picture? The answer suddenly became apparent. Our technology was not lagging so far behind as the experts would have us believe. There simply had been no economic incentive before the winter of '73-4 to contemplate seriously the rapid development of alternate energy sources for mass production. We were struggling along quite comfortably on the old technology, heating our homes with crude oil and tooling around the countryside in gasoline-powered cars. Then the floor fell out from under us, for the reasons already discussed, and an economic vacuum was created. A new profit incentive entered the arena. A market had quickly emerged for alternate fuel sources and, as we mentioned in an earlier section, industry always moves in to fill an economic vacuum. It is this basic economic law, perhaps more than any other factor, which puts the lie to the Doomsday Brigade and its gloomy scenarios. Just when conditions appear to be at their worst, and our entire civilization seems ready to collapse around our heads, a new set of variables is created which further accelerates the rate of progress.

Instead of fearing crises, we should welcome them. For they are only temporary setbacks which invariably jolt us out of our lethargy and spur us on to greater levels of achievement. Every collapse of the old technology hastens the development of something new and better. Progress is being made in the areas of solar and fusion energy, and also the production of synthetic fuels, geothermal power, magnetohydrodynamic plants, and energy from winds and tides. By 1984 the energy crisis is likely to be totally eliminated from the Doomsday Brigade's arsenal of scenarios.

5

Solar energy. The technology is ready to be implemented. Just how soon are we likely to have it on a broad scale? The answer depends, once again, largely on government policies in the area.

According to Peter E. Glaser, vice president of Arthur D. Little, Inc., "within a year [by summer, 1975], we shall see several of the solar demonstration projects currently underway confirming to the public that the technology for solar-heated and -cooled buildings is workable. During the time these demonstrations are in progress, industry should be able to identify a market which will justify building up the capability to mass-produce, at competitive costs, the systems and components required for solar space heating and cooling. . . .

"We believe that one of the most effective ways to advance the time when solar energy will be used on a wide scale is for the government to create incentives which concentrate on market factors. . . . Before making major investments, industry needs to be assured that, as its manufacturing and inventory investment in solar-powered equipment develops, there will be a continuity of government policy. . . . The building owner needs to be assured that his investment in a solar climate-control system will not mean an increase in his real estate tax . . . most of all [industry] needs a consistent government policy so it can plan its future actions."

A consistent government policy so industry can plan its future actions. Industry needs to be assured it will not be penalized with rising taxes and other arbitrary legislation once it has invested huge sums of money in solar energy. This is the key to the time factor. How soon can we have solar energy on a large scale? Within the next few years if the politicians do not create a climate hostile to its development. Rooftop solar stoves used to heat water already exist in Australia, Israel, Japan, and in some sections of the United States, and the generation of solar electricity is not too far off. Two astronomers at the University of Arizona, Aden and Marjorie Meinel, have designed what they call "solar farms" using metal plates which absorb and trap the sun's heat for the production of pollution-free electric power. The Meinels foresee a day when a network of these farms span seventy-five square miles of the southwestern desert generating enough power to satisfy the needs of the entire country.

Even if this becomes feasible within the next decade, however, we would probably not want to depend completely on a single energy source for all our power. A breakdown in the network would cripple the country if we had no other alternatives to take up the slack. The best course for us in the near future is to develop four or five power sources so we can have a better understanding of the advantages and disadvantages of all of them, and avoid putting ourselves at the mercy of a paralyzing collapse in any one area. With this goal in mind, the Rogers Engineering Company has prepared a site for a geothermal energy station in Marysville, Montana. Drilling began in the summer of 1974. The idea of drilling a hole to extract heat from the earth is not particularly new. Italy started harnessing geothermal energy in 1904, and it has also been done in Iceland, Japan, New Zealand, and in Sonoma County, California, ninety miles northeast of San Francisco. Here, steam is released from geyser fields deep in the earth, and channeled into turbogenerators producing over three hundred thousand kilowatts of electricity—enough to satisfy approximately 40 percent of San Francisco's energy needs.

But in Montana, the attempt will be made for the first time to tap the heat of dry hot rock in the earth rather than steam fields. Geologists believe that "hot rock reservoirs" exist throughout the western United States, with a potential energy reserve equal to our total coal deposits. William R. McSpadden, a research scientist with the project, claims that a cubic mile of hot rock can yield a billion dollars worth of energy at current market prices. If this experiment is successful, industries will move in to take advantage of cheap and abundant electric power, creating thousands of new jobs in an area where they are badly needed. There are a couple of questions that have to be answered before this happens, however. First, will the type of drilling and rock fracturing required here trigger earthquakes or, conversely, will it relieve stress in geological faults and prevent them from occurring? Second, is the energy-producing life of a geothermal field long enough to warrant the investment of huge sums of capital in the first place? The operation in Montana should answer these basic questions, and possibly uncover valuable new energy sources within the next few years.

Also being discussed now is the possibility of harnessing the energy in the winds and tides. By constructing giant windmills on floating platforms in the ocean, sufficient power can be generated to obtain hydrogen from sea water to supplement oil, natural gas, and coal as a fuel source. It could be burned directly in stoves, hot water heaters, furnaces, and automobiles (when mixed with powdered metal hydrides)—and the water vapor it gives off is extremely clean. Right now hydrogen is expensive, but mass production would lower the price, and modern methods of handling it make it safe to use. Tidal energy, too, is a cheap and pollution-free alternative currently being exploited off the coast of Brittany in France. The winds and tides will never be a major power source for two reasons—the fickleness of the elements combined with the necessary remoteness of power stations from the consumer—but they will certainly be used as valuable supplements in the not-too-distant future.

What else? Synthetic fuels. Glenn C. Werth, a physicist at the Lawrence Livermore Laboratory in California, thinks it may be possible to create methane in the earth by forcing oxygen and water into fractured coal seams for less money than we are now paying for imported natural gas. A more expensive method calls for the artificial production of hydrocarbon through coal gasification, and the manufacture of oil by shale mining in our western states—an alternative violently opposed by the ecologists because of its inevitable impact on the landscape. Then there is a system for improving the efficiency of fossil fuel plants by passing ionized steam rapidly through a magnetic field (magneto-hydrodynamics). An estimated 20 percent more electricity can be generated from the same quantity of fuel once this system is perfected, say researchers in the field.

All in all, the worldwide energy picture presented in the bleak winter of '73 and '74 is changing drastically.

Alternatives are proliferating like rabbits. Planet earth, apparently entering the beginning of a new Dark Age not so long ago, is now blazing with energy and vitality. A moribund industry is rejuvenated. Capitalists from all countries are stepping in to make the world safe for the Doomsday Brigade, and will rake in handsome profits while they are at it. The profit motive—that wicked desire to earn money—will obliterate another doomsday scenario if it is permitted to run amuck in the energy markets of the world.

6

And then there will be fusion. Nuclear fusion started with fission. It started with the splitting of the atom which released incredible amounts of energy previously believed to be unattainable. In nuclear fusion atoms are fused together instead of split. Fusion is better than fission since it produces hardly any radioactive byproducts, whereas we still do not know how to store properly all the radioactive wastes produced in fission. Thermal pollution—heated water discharged into rivers and lakes by nuclear fission plants—renders our fish inedible and could lead to the evolution of biological monstrosities over the years. Fusion, on the other hand, offers the promise of clean, inexpensive, and unlimited energy. As such, it seems right now to be the final long-range answer to the energy requirements of the human race.

Thermonuclear fusion is the process which fires the sun (and all the other stars) with the combination of hydrogen atoms to produce heavier atoms of helium. This is the same process used in a hydrogen bomb, as opposed to the atom bomb which is triggered by fission. The problem of controlling this natural activity of the sun and stars in a laboratory, however, had been considered beyond human solution at our present level of development. As late as May 1973, the consensus of most American scientists working in the field was that fusion power "will probably not be available as an energy source for decades to come." The ability to control the temperature and pressure needed to fuse together heavy hydrogen atoms such as deuterium and tritium in order to create helium atoms was something which would finally be achieved by our great-great-grandchildren. The highest temperature reached in a controlled laboratory situation by May 1973 was 12.5 million degrees Fahrenheit, while the temperature required for a fusion reaction is 180 million degrees. Progress had been substantial, but there was still too far to go to think about perfecting the process in the foreseeable future.

Less than a year later, in May 1974, KMS Industries, Inc., of Ann Arbor, Michigan, announced a significant breakthrough. KMS had succeeded in releasing high-energy particles called neutrons with the help of a laser beam. The fusion reaction had only lasted a short while but, nonetheless, the event was heralded as a "significant initial step" toward the production of sustained fusion energy. Dr. Keeve M. Siegel, chairman of KMS Industries, claimed that the experiment in laser-generated fusion had been conducted successfully on four occasions—May 1st and 3rd, and twice on May 9th. It was generally regarded as the first time it had been done anywhere on earth. While this was taking place, different scientists reported substantial progress in another means of producing fusion energy: the containment of heated gas known as plasma in a magnetic field.

A spokesman for KMS Industries predicted that we could now expect to be manufacturing fusion energy commercially by the early 1980s. Most important of all, this achievement has been accomplished without any government financing whatsoever. As such, it is a splendid example of how major improvements in the human condition can be made without massive infusions of public funds. The resources are already out there in the marketplace, notwithstanding the huge tax bite the politicians are taking out of private paychecks and corporate profits. How much more would be available if government left the money where it belonged in the first place—with the people who earned it—instead of funneling it to Washington, D.C., where a substantial part of it is devoured by the federal bureaucracy?

We will be forced to depend on the old energy technology for only a few years longer instead of the thirty-to-eighty-year period accepted only a couple of years ago. This is a far more promising picture than the Doomsday Brigade was painting for us in the winter of America's most severe energy crisis. The sun. The wind. The tides. Fusion. Heat from the earth itself. The future will be upon us before we know it.

Meanwhile, we can take comfort from the figures published by the American Petroleum Institute in July 1974. Supplies of major oil products, including heating oil, "are much higher now than a year ago," the report claimed. Inventories of jet fuel were up 25 percent, automobile gasoline almost 10 percent, and heating oil 15 percent.

Six months earlier we were on the brink of Doom. Eternal shortages. Collapse. Despair.

And then abundance.

The Doomsday Brigade was shot down once again. Headed off at the pass by the forces of progress. But never fear. The pessimists will be back tomorrow with a new scenario filled with lurid visions of death and destruction.

7

Overpopulation. Famine. Pollution. Energy shortages. One by one the Doomsday Brigade is running short on crises. What will it come up with next to titillate the fancies of necrophiles the world over?

Um . . . let's see now. Invasion from Jupiter? Too kinky. The public is unsophisticated, but not quite dumb enough to go for that one. Not after being had already by Orson Welles. Mutants? Psychopathic robots? A giant fungus run amuck in the streets of New York City? Revolutionary dolphins taking over amusement parks, eventually the world?

Too science fictiony. Where oh where is the next doomsday scenario going to come from?

Stay tuned here for the next episode.

BOOK TWO

Here Comes 1984

VII

The Growth of the Multinationals

1

Here you are in the world of 1984.

Big Brother? Something has gone wrong. What we have in reality is the mirror-image of the society portrayed in George Orwell's novel. Data banks? Telescreens? Of course they exist. But, as Nicholas von Hoffman put it in a remarkably perceptive column, the tables have been turned; instead of government spying on the public, "we know everything about the government." The new technology, created by the private sector, works *on behalf of the public* rather than the despots who seek to control it for their own ends.

During the decade extending from 1974 to 1984, the politicians became more and more entangled in their own bureaucracy. It was a question of the inherent inefficiency of the bureaucrats as opposed to the efficacy of the marketplace. The television cameras have been turned around, the data banks reprogrammed to tell us more about our elected officials. Already in 1974 we had a society where we knew all the intimate details about the private lives of politicians—who contributed to their campaign funds, how much, when, in cash or in checks, what type of mental treatment they received in the past (as in the case of the almost-vice presidential candidate of the Democratic Party in 1972), with whom they spent their weekends, what they did, what kind of furs and jewels their wives wore, where they got them, what schools their children went to, on and on ad infinitum.

This is the "antithesis of the all-seeing telescreen" in Orwell's *1984*, said Nicholas von Hoffman in 1974. How right he was. Government knows less and less about the citizenry while we, the people, know every conceivable thing there is to know about a candidate for public office.

The trend started in the early 1970s—oh, before that really, in the twilight years of the sixties—and proved irreversible. At some point in that period a new kind of aristocracy emerged. It was a natural outgrowth of the electronic era. With the birth of television and instantaneous communication, celebrities were suddenly idolized like royalty in earlier centuries. It did not matter what kind of fame one had achieved. Politicians, gangsters, movie stars, sports heroes, even a handful of authors were all lumped into the same category; they were *famous*. All the public responded to was their comparative levels of celebrity. The more exalted they were, the more the public wanted to know about them. The idea was to *become* famous and *stay* famous; who cared how? The price of fame was loss of privacy. The public demanded intimacy with the celebrated. Movie stars were able to camouflage their private lives a bit to make themselves appear more glamorous. Politicians, attempting the same thing, were tossed in jail for perjury.

Those who had become celebrities in one profession were able to slip into other fields with amazing agility. Famous movie stars became famous governors; famous mayors like John Lindsay of New York City became actors (not such a drastic change when you stop to think about it), while other former politicians and sports figures went into broadcasting. It did not matter what one did for a living, really, so long as he kept his name before the public. And those aspiring to fame understood the price they had to pay: bugs hidden under the wallpaper, zoom-lens cameras observing them from a building three blocks away while they ate; phones tapped at all hours while they arranged a rendezvous with their concubines. In short, they were forced to become public figures in the literal sense of the term: their lives were shorn of every semblance of privacy. Politicians were scrutinized all the more carefully because they wielded power over the lives of others. After all, a celebrity like Willie Mays never taxed anyone or built a monument to himself with someone else's money.

Big Brother in 1984? The United States and most of the civilized world resembles a gargantuan television studio instead, and our public figures are the leading players constantly on stage before the multitudes.

2

While this trend was evolving through the 1970s, governments grew more and more ineffectual in handling international crises. Periodic brushfire wars would flare up—Turkey *vs.* Greece one year, Pakistan *vs.* India another, Tanzania *vs.* the Congolese Republic yet again—and, since most politicians were either in jail or under indictment, there was precious little they could do to ease the situation. A vacuum was created. Who was going to fill it? Tuccille's First Law of Reality—industry always moves in to fill an economic vacuum—took effect once again. Those with the most to lose (that's who) stepped in to save the day. Multinational corporations, with investments in every conceivable nook and cranny of the planet, simply could not tolerate the prospect of small wars escalating into big ones.

War is bad for business, bad for profits. It upsets the rhythmic flow of the marketplace.

So it happened that the multinationals emerged as the principal force for peace and progress in the latter half of the 1970s. To be sure, there had been substantial resistance to them earlier in the decade. The United Nations, recognizing that the multinationals were evolving into a dominant force in the world arena, could not stand the competition and held meetings in 1972 and 1973 calling for restraints. American unions, particularly the AFL-CIO, also called for congress to "adopt regressive protectionist measures that would curtail foreign investment," according to Walter E. Schirmer, chairman of the Clark Equipment Company, in an address at Duquesne University on July 6, 1973. The unions claimed that multinational corporations manufactured products overseas and imported them into the United States, thus upsetting our balance-of-trade position and depriving the American work force of needed jobs. Yet, as Schirmer pointed out, this was not the case. A study conducted by the Department of Commerce revealed that the multinationals had actually increased their domestic employment by 31 percent over a ten-year period, while purely national corporations increased employment only 12 percent. The multinational corporations, with plants operating overseas, had to build subsidiary factories in the United States to supply their foreign plants with necessary parts and equipment. The net result had been a growth in both exports and jobs at home, while national and international firms were lagging behind in both categories.

(Definitions: national companies are those manufacturing and marketing their products in one country; internationals are those manufacturing at home but selling their goods in more than one country; multinationals have plants all over the world, and usually hire local labor for manufacturing, merchandising, and sales.)

This being the case, why did the unions oppose the new multinationals which were generating additional jobs in the American marketplace? If the unions had succeeded in stifling their growth, the prime victims would have been the very workers the unions represented. George W. Ball, former under-secretary of state, zeroed in on the real reason in a speech before the National Industrial Conference Board in early 1973: "It is the fear that this new mobility of industry will erode their bargaining position that has, in my view, led the AFL-CIO to embark on a shrill campaign against multinational companies with arguments logically unsustainable."

In a nutshell: loss of power. If a corporation shifts its production facilities *within* a country, the unions can and do follow. But they do not have any bargaining power for workers hired in Belgium or Mozambique. Deliberately ignored by opponents of the multinational corporation was the fact that other nations were building plants in the United States at the same time. Companies in Japan, Germany, England, Switzerland, and other industrial countries were investing capital and equipment in various areas of the world, including America, creating new jobs and contributing to worldwide economic growth. Multinationalism is not a one-way street, and never was. Everyone benefits from it, and always did.

No matter, though.

The United Nations viewed the multinationals as a threat to its prestige; dictatorial governments saw them as liberators of their own oppressed subjects; and unions feared them because of an alleged challenge to their bargaining power—and they all joined together to cripple them in their infancy.

To no avail, however. Economic multinationalism was an idea whose time had come. Historical forces were at work. The rate of progress could be slowed temporarily, but not completely stopped.

3

"The prospect of world war is becoming more and more unthinkable," says Richard Bode, a free-lance writer specializing in new technology. "The old cliché, World Peace Through World Trade, sounds kind of corny, but its becoming a reality just the same. Already we're moving beyond world trade into the next phase," he said in 1974. "What's developing is an interlocking corporate structure on a world scale. We're all becoming investors in everyone else's economy. War, hell! The multinational corporations can't *afford* a major war. They'll do everything they can to avoid one."

Richard Bode was not alone in recognizing the multinationals as an emerging force for world peace in 1974. Historian Arnold Toynbee made the same observation in a magazine article, adding that they were the healthiest force on earth while oppressive political regimes were growing more rickety and inefficient. Critics of the multinationals expressed the fear that they were becoming so powerful they could flout the laws of individual nations and operate with impunity like latter-day pirates, but it soon became apparent that these corporations were better citizens than the local political rulers themselves. More often than not, they were inclined to observe local laws and customs to the last dotted "i" since they had investments to protect. If they were tossed out of a country for any reason, they lost access to a valuable market. By and large, the countries which complained the most about economic colonialism and capitalist exploitation were the ones gaining the most through increased employment and material benefits where none previously existed. Historically, tinhorn dictators have duped the masses into believing only they could deliver them from poverty and starvation. The multinationals produced results rather than flowery but empty rhetoric. The quality of life was improved by the only power on earth capable of doing the job: private investment capital from all over the world. The catalyst was money; the result: economic activity, jobs, industrialization, and a quick ascent from primitivism toward the twenty-first century. As the multinationals spread their network of investments across the globe, the power of nations to wage war gradually diminished.

World peace—the bright elusive dream that had eluded mankind since the beginning of recorded history—seemed within our grasp by the late 1970s.

4

The force that made the multinational company a reality was technology. In the past a corporation had to be a compact structure. It had to have access to banks, postal service, factories, and customers. Physical proximity was mandatory. Time was valuable and both communication and delivery were drawn-out affairs. The telephone helped spread things out a bit; electronics made it possible for a company to expand its facilities throughout a nation. But the corporation remained primarily a national institution. Postal service was slow and you could do only so much business over the telephone.

Then the computer came along and changed all that. Telecommunications and teleprocessing revolutionized the world economy. Geography ceased to be of importance.

No longer was it necessary to be physically near facilities. Suddenly, the entire planet was "near." By the early 1970s information was transmitted everywhere on earth in seconds, via teletype machines and communications satellites. It was possible to make airline and hotel reservations anywhere on the planet by calling a single toll-free number. Brokerage houses no longer had to send pieces of paper from place to place. Stocks and bonds remained in a central vault while credits and debits were toted electronically on personal accounts. A single corporation could be strewn across the globe while its various divisions communicated with one another as though located in one building. As technology developed in different parts of the planet—the rotary engine in West Germany, cash-dispensing terminals in England, computers in the United States, magnetic tape facilities in Japan—the information was transferred instantaneously by multinational corporations with cross-licensing contracts.

Information was shared instantly.

Technology was implemented globally for everyone's benefit.

Secrecy, never desirable in the first place, was no longer possible. The spontaneous exchange of talent, genius, and technology generated an economic revolution unprecedented in human history. By 1977, Western-style affluence had already made significant inroads in much of South America. The newer African nations were industrializing heavily by 1980. Today, May 30, 1984 (my birthday as it turns out; I will not say which one since age is no longer important), famine and overpopulation have been eliminated as serious threats throughout most of Asia.

The only societies on earth still suffering from poverty and hunger are the handful of dictatorships remaining, particularly those with a socialist economy. The Soviet Union remains committed to its outmoded Marxist ideology, although some of the party leadership has been clamoring behind the scenes for capitalist reforms. Albania is still fairly primitive, and Greece has so far failed to recapture even a semblance of its former grandeur. India has made considerable progress in the past ten years, but backslides periodically because of an uncontrollable mania for nationalizing its major industries. Of the European nations, England lags behind the continent with its Labor government persisting in its usual debilitating policies and the Conservatives offering ineffectual opposition.

By and large, however, the bulk of the planet has gone over to a more-or-less market economy. The Arabs, having abandoned socialism in the mid-seventies, have proved themselves *nonpareil* capitalists with a particularly aggressive bent. The ethic of the ancient bazaar is remarkably effective in an advanced economy. They now trade fission energy and miracle food with the same admirable abandon they once swapped oil, hand-loomed rugs, and beads. Mainland China, a struggling Communist slave camp ten short years ago, now vies with the Arabs for the "Profiteers-of-the-Eastern-Hemisphere" award. Israel has been transformed into the entertainment capital of the world by Prime Minister Sammy Davis, Jr., who has been in office for the past six years. Japan enjoys preeminence with the United States, West Germany, and Oceana I (an ocean community developed by Disney Enterprises) as one of the most productive economic powers on earth.

"So it goes," said Kurt Vonnegut a generation ago. And so it goes today throughout most of the planet earth. Multinationals. Investments. Economic dynamism. And rising affluence. The free market ethic is spreading. Those refusing to embrace it are doing so at their own peril.

5

"The multinational company has the capacity to diminish the power of centralized government—indeed, perhaps even to distribute power more equitably throughout the world," said Walter E. Schirmer in 1974. His projection at the time turned out to be amazingly prescient. Political structure has changed considerably in the freer nations of the world. In the United States we have seen the emergence of a third major political party—The Libertarian Party—which grows increasingly stronger. A congressional coalition of Libertarians and economy-minded Republicans and Democrats has successfully stymied government spending and reduced federal taxing power. Americans also enjoy more basic freedoms today than the citizens of any other nation. With the virtual elimination of world war, poverty, and hunger as a threat to domestic peace, the United States is more at rest with itself than at any time in the recent past. Dissension exists on all fronts, to be sure, but it is generally of a nonviolent nature. Much remains to be done, but evolution has replaced revolution as the means of change.

Elsewhere the pattern is similar to the United States. Major political leaders in Europe and the rest of the developing world grow less and less enamored of socialism and more convinced of the efficacy and justice of the free market. Facts have finally begun to speak louder than words, and the masses of earth are no longer satisfied with demagogic rhetoric; they demand visible results in the form of food, housing, and other material benefits. In general terms, the marketplace has replaced the seat of government as the focal point of human energy and activity, and the trend continues at an accelerating rate.

Heads of state are frequent guests on television talk shows, and they regularly participate in those celebrity tennis matches that became so popular back in the 1960s. They also golf a good deal on weekends, usually in the company of movie and television stars. They are invited on fishing and skiing trips by wealthy singers and industrialists, and otherwise made to feel important by the productive elements of society. By and large, their salaries are still paid out of public tax funds—much the same as the Queen of England used to receive an allowance at the forbearance of the English public. But their power is not the same as it used to be. Their position is increasingly a figurehead one. They are called in as consultants by representatives of industry and labor, but this is more a goodwill gesture than anything else. For the most part, the decisions that affect our lives are made in the markets of the world. Our political leaders are tolerated and, in some cases, venerated just so long as they do not upset the general standard of living. Like that old plug-in TV console in the attic we just can't bring ourselves to toss out with the rubbish, we like to keep our politicos around more out of a sense of nostalgia than anything else.

6

The specific technology which helped elevate the multinational corporation to its current level of importance is the data bank. Once feared by civil libertarians as a threat to individual privacy, data banks have long since proved themselves to be one of the most liberating influences on the human condition. The original fear they provoked was genuine. The computerization of information on individuals and organizations determined their credit standing; erroneous or incomplete data could unjustly destroy someone's ability to operate effectively in a credit-oriented society. But these potential dangers were eliminated by a Comprehensive Right to Privacy Act (jointly sponsored by both conservative and liberal legislators with libertarian leanings in this area) in the mid-1970s. This act granted every citizen the right to inspect his file; supplement it with additional information; delete information which was demonstrably false; prohibit the disclosure of personal data to unauthorized personnel; keep a record of all those with access to the files; and other safeguards designed to protect his privacy and security.

As it turned out, computerized data banks afforded the public a greater degree of privacy than the old technology ever did. In the past virtually everyone with a proper set of burglar's tools and the ability to use them could steal paper files locked in someone's office. The information was printed on paper and sorted in file folders for anyone with a third-grade education to read. The new technology changed all that. No longer could private information be stolen. Computers are coded, and only a handful of individuals who know the necessary codes and passwords, and possess the right electronic "badges," can extract information. In addition, we know exactly who they are. Any data leaked to unauthorized sources can be traced back through a chain of command. The computers, themselves, are guarded in hidden vaults which can be reached only by performing an elaborate routine known to a select few. The individual, and the detailed data on his life, is far better protected here than he was by the technology of print and paper file folders. This development alone is of revolutionary importance.

Even more significant, however, is the amount of data which can now be stored. We have a data-rich economy, with literally *millions of times more* valuable information at our fingertips than was previously possible. In the field of medicine, all the vital information about an individual's medical history is available on a moment's notice. The names of those all over the country with rare blood types can be produced in seconds, and a donor flown to the bedside of a dying patient. A parent whose child swallows a household detergent can call the nearest Poison Control Center and learn the exact chemical ingredients and the proper antidote; doctors relied largely on guesswork before. In business a company's total assets are inventoried and necessary purchases made automatically by computers programmed for the task. Computers save us months and years of research by performing complex calculations in the wink of an eye. We are moving from a credit society toward an accounting society. Purchases are made at department stores and supermarkets while computers make the appropriate deductions from our personal accounts. Weeks of book-keeping are done in miniseconds. The need for paperwork—paper money, paper checks, paper invoices—is being phased out with swift dispatch.

The effect of data banks on multinationals has been nothing short of phenomenal. At one point in the early 1970s it became physically impossible for human beings to keep track of the myriad cross-licensing contracts among the various multinational corporations. Today, if IBM wants to learn the precise dollars-and-cents relationship between itself and Sony regarding a specific contract, a computer spews forth all the pertinent data in seconds. No more searching through file cabinets for elusive contracts, and poring endlessly through impenetrable legal documents. Data banks give us instant access to collected information and speed up the decision-making process. Trade agreements which once took weeks and months to formulate are now worked out in minutes. Because of this factor alone we are able to transfer necessary goods and services to the consumer in a fraction of the time formerly required. Fifty thousand pages of information are stored on a four-by-six inch plastic card, eliminating thousands of cubic feet of storage space a company formerly had to set aside. Miniature "file cabinets" the size of a sugar cube store trillions of statistics, architectural drawings, computer data, photographs, maps, and other pertinent material. These lithium niobate crystals are rotated in laser beams and desired information is projected onto a screen for viewing. The storage space previously required for this amount of information was a structure larger than the Empire State Building. We have literally reached the point where an executive can go off on a business trip with libraries full of information stacked neatly inside his suitcase. And the technology is still in its infancy. There are new developments every day. It is becoming more and more difficult to be a futurist. Scenarios projected five or ten years into the future transpire before the ink is dry on the page. Even the science fiction writers are having a bad time of it. Their most fanciful novels take on aspects of history textbooks by the time they reach the bookstores. It is a frustrating experience for all of us. We simply cannot keep abreast of new advances.

The pessimists have not retired, though. Paul Ehrlich was still doomsdaying through the early 1980s. Last week he predicted the total collapse of human civilization by February 30, 1985. When informed that February has only twenty-eight days in it, Ehrlich replied: "It doesn't matter. That's not important. My only concern is that humanity is doomed and nothing on earth can change that fact. The flood is coming. Americans must build an ark so the Fifth and Sixth World peoples can survive."

"How about us?" he was asked by a reporter. "Who's going to build an ark for us?"

"That's selfish and irresponsible," said Ehrlich. "Americans are the lepers of the solar system. The least we can do is take a dive and let the forest creatures inherit the earth."

VIII

The Leisure Class Society

1

Multinationals. Data banks. Leisure. The end of drudgery. In so many ways more and more of us are living like the aristocracy of earlier centuries. Within the past few years, the United States seems to have evolved from a predominantly middle-class into a leisure-class society. It was not so terribly long ago that the average man woke up with the sun and slaved away until after it settled beyond the western horizon for the night. His wife banged around in the house, baking bread and mending clothes until she was ready to drop with exhaustion. When they were not too tired to notice they were proud of what they made together, proud of the existence that would soon (too soon) send them bone-weary to the grave. They taught their children to work hard and get ahead because it was the only proper way to live. For generations there was no other alternative for the moral individual. If one believed in self-sufficiency and achieving what he could on his own merits (insofar as was humanly possible), one worked and saved and made the most of a difficult existence. Only a few—a select few—were able to lead a life of cultured leisure for reasons which had little to do with talent or capability.

After a while the working classes decided they had had enough. Revolutions were launched with varying degrees of success against the aristocracies of England and France. The most successful of these—the Revolution of 1776—ushered in a different age which made upward mobility a real possibility for the first time in modern history. This new Age of Man and Reason did away with the old restrictions based on birth and class. The New Age created an ethic founded on individualism and freedom (imperfectly applied, unfortunately, because of the continuation of slavery) and made it possible for a more open kind of society to emerge: a meritocracy of talent and genius. Individuals could suddenly rise or fall to a natural level among their fellow human beings in the give-and-take of a relatively free marketplace. Generally speaking, those with the best personal resources who applied themselves the hardest achieved the most in terms of wealth and self-satisfaction. Those with fewer talents and less determined effort were not so successful, in a material sense at least. This ethic came to be known by several names. Some called it individualism; others referred to it as the Protestant work ethic; while a few (like William Graham Sumner and H. L. Mencken) were not ashamed to label it Social Darwinism.

Individualism, as we have already noted in Section II, sustained a major political and philosophical assault in the United States beginning near the end of the nineteenth century and lasting throughout the first two-thirds of the twentieth century. Though it was badly adulterated by hostile legislation, an innate American streak of basic common sense (Paine was right on target in so many ways) enabled us to weather the storm and reestablish individualism as the dominant force in American life during the late 1970s. We left the old industrial age behind and launched a new technological revolution which proved even more liberating than those preceding it. This revolution owes some of its heritage to Thomas Aquinas who had established the principle, before the Protestant Reformation, that work should provide man with dignity as well as material rewards. He was deeply concerned about shortening the workday and making labor as pleasant as possible so everyone would want to indulge in it. For centuries this dream was impossible to fulfill. Work, for the most part, was long and tedious; it was performed out of necessity in an effort to survive. Now, after an eternity of long drudging labor, the human race is well on its way toward shortening the workday and workweek to a degree Aquinas never dreamed was possible.

2

One of the first major moves in this direction occurred in the spring of 1972 when the Thomas J. Lipton Company inaugurated a three-day workweek at its packing plants in Galveston, Texas, Albion, New York, and Flemington, New Jersey. Instead of working the usual seven hours a day, five days a week, Lipton employees were put on a twelve-hours-a-day, three-days-a-week schedule. The idea was to follow a growing trend toward a shorter workweek so the American worker could enjoy the benefits of a longer weekend. More time for play and leisure, less time spent in labor. One more step along the road to freedom.

In most cases Lipton employees were ecstatic with the new arrangement. Wives welcomed the opportunity for their husbands to spend more time with them and the children, while those same husbands had other ideas about how to spend their extra holidays each week.

"More time to go fishing and camping. More time to relax and enjoy life. More time to get away from it all," was the typical reaction of men who saw the leisure-time bonus as a chance to spend more time *away* from home rather than with their families. (Alas, we all have different notions of Utopia—one more reason why it is impossible to achieve.)

While the majority of workers welcomed the three-day week, there was a vocal minority who insisted the old way was better: working parents whose three-day shifts were on alternating cycles, meaning they stopped seeing each other altogether; nervous wives with thirsty husbands who entertained visions of four-day nonstop benders ending in the gutter; and those who resist change at any time because the slightest alteration in their lives is more than they can handle. There is probably a hidden faction that is totally perplexed about not having anyone telling it what to do for four consecutive days. (What *does* one do with all that time, when he has been accustomed to taking orders all his life?)

Despite the negative reaction from some, there was no question that the move toward a shorter workweek was a growing trend. Company officials generally claimed that the concentration of working hours resulted in increased efficiency, a decline in lateness and absenteeism, and higher employee morale. Society benefited from midweek "weekends" which reduced normal weekend traffic and congestion at beaches and parks. Single people, particularly, were most enthusiastic about being able to skip away to ski resorts and singles excursions on minivacations every week.

In 1974, figures revealed that approximately a thousand companies across the country had adopted the three- or four-day workweek, and thousands more were planning to do so. In *Things To Come,* Herman Kahn and B. Bruce-Briggs projected that we would establish the "leisure society" well before the year 2000. We would all be paid much more for fewer hours of work made more productive by computerized machines (cybernetics), and this growing affluence would free us finally from the drudgery of the past. The three days spent on the job each week have already been sliced from twelve- to ten-hour workdays in most cases. Conceivably, the average man may spend no more than twenty to twenty-four hours laboring each week before the century is out.

(There is some speculation by the more cynical among us that he doesn't work more than three or four hours in an eight-hour workday anyway.)

3

True to form, the pessimists predicted all sorts of chaos if the common man suddenly found himself with so much leisure time on his hands. These projections were based on the concept that most people did not understand the nature of leisure in the first place. In *Of Time, Work, and Leisure*, Sebastian de Grazia made the point that leisure should not be confused with free time. Free time, badly spent, is not leisure but simply time wasted, according to de Grazia. Quoting heavily from Greek and Roman authors, he maintained that a man is leisurely only when he is free. A prisoner has all sorts of time on his hands, but that is different from having leisure time. Leisure is freedom from clocks to do the things we want to do. It is time spent creatively, or at least voluntarily. Leisure is freedom from the *necessity* of being occupied. (According to this definition, work done voluntarily for the pleasure and fulfillment it gives qualifies as leisure. Leisure does not eliminate work, only work done out of necessity.) To the Greeks and Romans—and later to de Grazia—the proper use of leisure is an art. It has to be learned and worked at.

It was probably true that much of the extra time gained

off the job initially was not really leisure in the Greek sense. We had a shorter work week, but the time spent away from work was taken up with other forms of drudgery: repairing homes and automobiles; standing in lines to renew drivers' licenses, buy fishing licenses, or even to go to a movie; checking out groceries in a supermarket; entertaining people we did not like for career reasons; attending obligatory social functions; fuming away in traffic jams. In many cases time spent off the job was not even free time. It was time eaten up by pressure and obligations. De Grazia took the apocalyptic view that leisure could be dangerous if a country did not know what to do with it. A society unprepared for leisure would grow decadent in times of prosperity. The result could be war and general violence. De Grazia's concern is well put and well received. It is the concern of a civilized man (one who knows how to use leisure properly) for the quality of life under changing conditions. Unlike the Doomsday Brigade, de Grazia's admonitions are rational and balanced.

Fortunately, man's inherent good sense prevailed once again. We did not become a society of drunkards and loafers. We diverted our energies into more constructive types of labor and recreation. Many people took second jobs to improve their economic standing in the community; others returned to school or turned to leisure-time activities (in the Greek and Roman sense) like tennis, golf, skiing, reading, chess, travel, music, hiking, and other pursuits offering both mental and physical benefits. The opportunity for voluntary work done for pleasure and fulfillment rather than necessity is possible for more people than ever before. We are beginning to experience a new renaissance in literature and music now that people have more time to develop talents that would have lain dormant in the past.

Yes, the doomsday prophets were wrong once again. The lie has been put over and over to their pessimistic (if not nihilistic) theories about the nature of man. And yet they will not go away; they will not be silent. They continue to hold their conferences at various universities several times a year. One by one they mount the podium and harangue the human race for crass stupidity and irresponsibility. Man is wicked; man is selfish; man is dense. Why *won't* the multitudes listen to us? Why won't the masses pay attention? They grow increasingly more shrill, in direct proportion to the declension of their following. Beastly common man! All he needs is a steeled, efficient dictator to drill some humility into his arrogant head.

4

While the time spent on the job each day and week diminishes, it also grows more pleasant because of the new technology. Office robots or minicarts have replaced the general factotum, delivering coffee, mail, and memos from one department to another. Nicknamed Marmaduke, after W. C. Fields' famous number-one amanuensis, this clever little machine tools around an office building along a network of magnetic wires hidden in the floors. It glides silently and is exceedingly polite, having been programmed to yield the right-of-way to its human coworkers. Besides delivering various items swiftly and efficiently, it also takes dictation without error or having to request repetition. The first models were invented by Customs Engineered Conveying Systems, headquartered in Detroit, and other firms offered competition soon afterward. Marmaduke is programmed to return by itself to a battery charging station when warning signals indicate it is running low on juice. Its major drawback is the fact it is not pleasant to look at. It has no legs worth ogling and fantasizing about. It is no fun to take out for a drink after work, or invite away for a secluded weekend at the seashore.

Another workday benefit of the new technology is BOSS, an electronic computer system developed by the

Honeywell Company which runs most new commercial buildings today. BOSS, more formally known as the Building Operation Service System, is designed to monitor air conditioning, heating, fire prevention, security, and other vital operations of a commercial building or complex of buildings. Entire cities will soon be hooked up to a central control system. Operational failures are picked up immediately by electronic sensors installed in a building's mechanical and electrical systems, and adjustments are made automatically. Countless lives and billions of dollars have been saved by reductions in fire and water damage, fuel leaks, and other breakdowns which were common only a decade ago. BOSS is the ultimate in mechanical slaves. He takes care of all our needs, keeps us comfortable, and protects us from harm. Unlike the benevolent dictators of the past, who promised us much the same in their quest for power, this BOSS can be easily neutralized once he begins to malfunction. He rules supreme only so long as the people want him to. Once he shows signs of becoming a trifle too uppity, it is no problem whatsoever to pull the plug and give him a lesson in modesty.

The drudgery of blue-collar labor has also been eliminated by industrial robots trained for drilling holes in metal, welding, knocking tin, lathing wire, spraying paint, and a host of jobs once described by Walter Reuther as "not worthy of human beings." The workmen who once performed these tasks are now employed as foremen over the machines. They order them about to their hearts' content, kick them in the rear if they fall down on the job, and call them "dummy" or "fathead" with impunity, which has resulted in incalculable psychological benefits for a formerly insecure species.

Other inventions of the past few years, including minicalculators, laser typewriters, and super copier machines, have all helped make the workday/workweek less laborious as well as shorter. Danger and occupational hazard have been removed from most forms of work. The net result has been an increase in leisure both *on* and *off* the job. Since working is more pleasant these days, it is performed with more enthusiasm. And work done voluntarily, as we mentioned a little earlier, also qualifies as leisure in the Greek sense of the word. Indeed, work and leisure are growing increasingly synonymous. If this trend continues, who can tell?—we may succeed in creating a truly civilized society after all.

5

With a superabundance of pessimists inflicting their dreary views on society, it is refreshing to come across one with a sense of humor. This saving grace qualifies Gore Vidal as my own favorite pessimist; he at least has the decency to present his nihilistic forecasts to the world with a certain elan. He amuses and entertains while he attempts to terrify us with pessimism. In the early 1970s he claimed the human race was destined to destroy itself with total decadence. "That's why I live in Rome," he added. "It's the most decadent place on earth." You have to admire a man with that kind of cavalier despair, not only for the future of the race, but his own fate as well. He definitely has style.

There was a certain nugget of truth to Vidal's ominous projection. He anticipated the affluent, leisure-class society before it came into existence, and realized how it would generate a hedonistic society as well. His mistake, however, was in equating hedonism with decadence. He failed to understand that hedonism was originally a creative concept which had been destroyed beyond all recognition over the centuries. It has gotten a bad press and, consequently, been maligned and misunderstood. Today it is usually identified with profligacy and dissolution.

For a more creative view of hedonism we are forced, once again, to turn back to our friends the Greeks. For them, pleasure was the primary good (to some the *only* good) in life. The individual fulfilled himself by pursuing pleasure and self-gratification. Epicurus regarded hedonism as a moral question, and taught that pleasure was the foundation of a moral man's entire life. While hedonism was later associated with dissipation, to the Greeks it meant just the opposite. The true Epicurean was expected to lead a life of prudent and restrained pleasure. He cultivated a taste for literature, wine, and music which elevated him above the herd. The difference between the Epicurean and the modern hedonist (at least as the public understands the word) is essentially the difference between the gourmet and the glutton.

The modern concept of hedonism owes more to Aristippus of Cyrene than to Epicurus. Aristippus, who preceded Epicurus by roughly a century, also maintained that pleasure was the primary end of life. But he was not so lofty as Epicurus about his notions of pleasure. Aristippus was more concerned about intense immediate pleasures which he held to be superior to any long-range concepts of cultivated refinement. Both Aristippus and Epicurus equated hedonism with the moral life and regarded self-denial as immoral.

Hedonism received strong support in the eighteenth century from the English Utilitarians Jeremy Bentham and James Mill, and later again from Mill's disciple-son, John Stuart Mill. The cornerstone of Utilitarianism was the belief that the purpose of life was the achievement of the greatest happiness for the greatest number of people. Bentham and his followers held that life was a tug-of-war between pleasure and pain, and the rational individual acted to increase the amount of pleasure and decrease the amount of pain he experienced in life. This sounds commonsensical enough, but these argumentative Englishmen saw fit to weave an entire philosophy around it. The ultimate goal for the Utilitarian was a life of total pleasure and the absence of pain and suffering, for society as well as himself.

Most people don't like to bother themselves about the

philosophical aspects of the things they do. Nevertheless, without thinking too much about it, we seem to be rediscovering the Epicurean concept of hedonism by trial-and-error. The old symbols of hedonism—the drunk, the glutton, the libertine—are now recognized for what they are: not hedonists at all, but rather unstable neurotics rebelling against society in a manner which produces pain instead of pleasure. They represent, in fact, the very antithesis of hedonism. Today we are beginning to move closer and closer toward a society of rational hedonism, toward a life of creative and constructive pleasure and away from self-punishment, self-sacrifice, and general self-destruction. We are learning to pursue pleasure for the first time without feeling guilty about it. We are learning to accept pleasure as a natural condition of life, not something to be earned after a lifetime of hardship and denial. The hedonistic society conceived of by the ancient Greeks should soon be ours, a natural adjunct to the society of leisure and pleasant labor.

The average American lives as well as the leisure class of earlier centuries. His home is no mansion, to be sure, but comes equipped with conveniences the old aristocracy never imagined possible. Most of our homes are better lit and better heated than the mansions of the past. Many are filled with expensive silverware, good food, and decent wine. We have closets full of clothing and mechanical servants which perform more efficiently and honestly than the human variety (and larceny never enters their brain centers). Middle class children today are at least more practically educated (no futile classicism with this generation) than were the scions of the old leisure class. By 2000 A.D. we will all live more lavishly and leisurely than even the wealthy live today.

6

There is no question that pessimism can be attractive, especially when one is hungover or in a particularly rotten mood. Yet, sustained pessimism is self-defeating and demoralizing. Sooner or later the hangover has to end, the mood must change for the better. Nothing less than our collective sanity is at stake. If the freedom to make choices is the *sine qua non* of morality, then optimism is the only state possible for the sane and rational individual. It is impossible to operate effectively otherwise. And so we recognize the outside chance that man will fail to learn the lessons of history and repeat the mistakes of the past. We indulge the Gore Vidals from time to time because they are amusing, because they warn us cleverly against the baser aspects of our nature. At the same time we dare not consider too seriously their notions about man's innate decadence or depravity. We entertain and pamper nihilism at our own risk, for pessimism is the very root, the very essence of totalitarianism. It is a philosophy founded in despair, and its ultimate path is a dead-end street ending in darkness and human savagery.

The human condition improves because it must improve. Our technology, our spreading affluence, our creative leisure are ongoing testimonials to the genius of man. Our potential is infinite and only optimism can fulfill it. The race of man is surviving, in most areas prospering. We pamper amusing pessimists occasionally, but we dare not let them interfere with the important work at hand.

IX

The Things They Thought Of Next

1

"What will they think of next?" was an old cliché-question asked over and over again during the middle-third of this century. Starting roughly with the advent of television, we entered an era where the human race was bombarded with new inventions at an accelerating rate. Television. Fission. Transistors. Computers. Spaceships. Lasers. It was as though we had entered a time machine and found ourselves transported overnight to a strange world of the future. How could anyone possibly keep up with it? With one part of our mind we welcomed the new and different (it made life on earth so much more comfortable), while an atavistic voice within us stirred our sense of nostalgia, our fondness for things belonging to the past—rundown farmhouses in the country one could pick up for a song, potbellied stoves, gas lamps on the lawn, antiques of any and all descriptions. Yes, we welcomed the new and could not (cannot) conceive of doing without it. Yet, in our headlong rush toward the future, we were careful to preserve the best out of the past. The past and familiar was our security blanket as we confronted the unknown.

"What will they think of next?" I cannot pretend to know the answer to that question; I am not even sure who "they" are at this point. Apparently there is an army of magicians somewhere beyond my typewriter which keeps pulling amazing new trinkets out of a hat. But I do know that changes have occurred in our daily existence which are nothing short of phenomenal in the ten short years since I started this book. The gadgets we considered so dazzling and awe-inspiring back in 1974 are now hopelessly archaic. Indeed, many have already been retired to museums along with other antiques. It takes so little time for things to become antiques these days—four or five years where previously whole centuries were required.

Like many of my fellow human beings, I am simultaneously mesmerized and frightened by these developments. The conservative in me says slow down a bit; let us not throw out the baby with the bathwater in our quest for self-improvement; while the libertarian in me cries out for further examples of man's genius, additional conquests along the road toward the complete liberation of our species. Progress means freedom from all the tyrannies of the past—material and psychological as well as political. And yet we cannot totally obliterate the past. I hang on to old mementos: my high school yearbook, a twenty-year-old love letter, an old address book, an obsolete watch that ceased functioning when I was in college. I cannot bring myself to toss them out forever. I hold on to these ancient trappings and bring them with me wherever I go—the rusted and faded and stained paraphernalia of a day I shall never see again.

A day I never want to see again. But only relive, over and over, in reverie, during private moments, when everyone else is asleep, and I am awake with only the ticking of a clock and a glass of brandy for company.

2

I am a hill of poetry. I am a bank of memories. And I am a thoroughgoing realist. I know that each step along the path of progress creates a new demand. The closer we get to perfection, the more impatient we become. We will never achieve perfection or Utopia, for we would have nothing left to aim for. The fun, you see, is in the striving. But, with every new advance, the multitudes grow more and more intoxicated with the prospect of finally attaining it, and this much is good. It stokes our curiosity. It inspires us to greater heights of achievement. The visible results of our efforts are incentives to keep on going, to see just how far we can travel before reaching the outer limits. We have attained a high level of creative leisure, but already it is not enough. Three years ago *yes,* but not today. Today we demand more and more of our technology.

This is 1984, and by 1975 we were already sick and tired of waiting as long as three seconds to get a dial-tone on the telephone. Three seconds! You could eat a hotdog with sauerkraut and relish (a whole meal) in three seconds. And that's not the only thing the public was fed up with. How about television sets that blew out a picture tube every ten thousand hours or so? The people didn't want to hear that mass-market television was scarcely thirty years old, or that the idea of transmitting pictures all the way around the world and into space was pure science fiction thirty-five years before. They were only concerned about the here and now, and fuzzy pictures, "snow," "ghosts," and echoes in the audio system simply could not be tolerated any longer.

What about wrist watches that had to be wound up

manually? Why couldn't "they" design a simple low-cost watch that wound itself up with the rhythm of the heartbeat? Or one that was completely trauma-proof—resistant to earthquakes, tidal waves, and muggings? Or one you could swim with, play handball with, skydive with, and wrestle alligators with? One you could drop off the roof of a forty-story building without damaging in any way? Why couldn't they do all that for $3.98? The public didn't want to hear about how our ancestors used to tell time with hourglasses and sundials, or by the movement of the sun and stars. The people wanted to know *exactly what time it is now*, and they didn't want any nonsense about it.

Why should it take as long as four minutes to get a series of complex calculations from a computer? Don't tell the public that the first crude computer was built as recently as 1939, that it weighed five tons and contained five hundred miles of wiring, and that by 1974 heuristic (learning) computers existed which were self-aware, self-correcting, and self-programming. The public didn't want to hear that these modern computers were capable of making millions of calculations a second. Why couldn't they make a billion, even a trillion calculations a second? People wanted answers *immediately*, and they grew impatient waiting four or five minutes for a dumb computer to spit them out.

What kind of society was it that manufactured stereophonic records that played only twenty minutes of music on each side; televisions that failed to provide play-back viewing on the demand of the viewer rather than the whim of the sender; cameras that took as long as fifteen seconds to develop a picture; golf balls that couldn't be found when you batted them into a jungle; showers where you had to regulate the water temperature yourself; double knit clothing that had to be pressed every six months; pocket calculators that were as bulky as a pack of cigarettes; deodorants that refused to protect us for longer than forty-eight hours of intensive tennis in the middle of August; trailers and campers that had to be plugged into an *external* electrical source; contact lenses and false teeth that had to be removed before we retired each night; typewriter ribbons that had to be replaced every three months?

No civilized society worth its name would tolerate outrages such as these any longer.

3

Yes, the law of rising expectations had us in its grip. We became more and more impatient with mechanical failure and inefficiency every day. We demanded increasingly more of the gadgets we developed to amuse ourselves—gadgets which, in most cases, would have seemed like pure magic a generation before. We could no longer settle for anything less than total freedom, not only from the tyrannies of the past, but also from every petty annoyance and inconvenience we could dream of.

We demanded a nuisance-free society to complement our unprecedented leisure—or else there was going to be hell to pay. Someone would have to answer for it.

In many ways our new inventions were obsolete hours after they hit the market. The human race lived in a fairly static world from its moment of birth until the end of the nineteenth century, and then found itself progressing in algebraic proportions. The title of Alvin Toffler's book, ***Future Shock***, became an integral part of our language instantaneously. People who never read the book knew immediately what he was talking about. We were being constantly bombarded with incredible new trinkets, and we no longer had to ask "What'll they think of next?" We had our answer every hour on the hour in our supercharged society. While the pessimists were warning us we would soon grow tired of our love affair with technology and revert to a simpler way of life, just the opposite occurred; we found we couldn't get enough. We were like children suddenly set loose in a toy factory. The more we saw the more we wanted. We refused to be sated, and our demands are now infinite. We can no longer wait for the future. We want the future now!

Fortunately, technology has been keeping pace with demand. By 1976 the television industry was subjected to revolutionary new changes. A gentleman named Henry Kloss of the Advent Corporation designed a wall-sized TV set for the home. The picture was projected onto a four-by-six feet screen on the wall, and the image was sharper than the tube picture. The sound was bounced off the screen by an audio console on the floor for a more realistic effect. The initial cost was fifteen hundred dollars, but our mass-marketing economy brought this down to a more acceptable level within a couple of years.

(Even as this was in the development stage, there were cries of indignation throughout the land: "Why a *screen* mounted on the wall? Why can't they build it *into* the wall? Why can't they custom-design it for the home? In cherrywood. In knotty pine. In stained walnut. Why can't they include it in the rent like air conditioning, wall ovens, dishwashers, washing machines, and wall-to-wall carpeting? Why can't they make it three-dimensional?")

Rest assured the television industry did everything it could to satisfy *all* the demands of the increasingly sophisticated consumer. A "telescopic ear" was developed which honed in on the conversations of quarterbacks, pitchers, and hockey players to provide the viewer with on-the-spot remarks made by their favorite sports heroes. ("Watch your language, Reggie. The *whole world* is listening.") Amazingly enough, these devices picked up sounds from five hundred feet away and filtered out all undesired background noise.

("Only *five* hundred feet away? Why not five *thousand? Fifty* thousand? Five *miles*?")

Discovision, Selectavision, Cartrivision, and Cassettavision are now standard commodities. Discovision is a play-back unit attached to the home television set which plays back desired portions of athletic contests (or any other program for that matter) on the demand of the viewer. Related to this is stop-action television, developed by Panasonic and Hitachi, which freezes selected frames on a smaller screen while action continues on the master screen. These were already available at popular prices by 1977. Selectavision, Cartrivision, and Cassettavision offer the public prerecorded programs which can be plugged into the home set; some are designed to supply the viewer with seven consecutive hours of entertainment.

("Why not all weekend? A *four-day* weekend?")

Those interested in the latest time-keeping instruments are wearing Patek Philippe watches with a self-adjusting calendar for leap year, and a more recent one made by Bulova which keeps us informed of the time, not only on earth, but on any planet of our choice. Others concerned merely about performance can buy a watch with a simplified gear system and antimagnetic parts made of plastic.

(As we can see, the old fear that the world was becoming more and more Americanized is long since passé. The Japanese, Swiss, Germans, and Oceanans are giving us stiff competition.)

4

Camera buffs have also been well provided for. The industrious Japanese invented a Vivitar lens camera which focuses clearly at all distances, and is lightweight and compact in the bargain. Another Japanese company has produced a zoom-lens videotape camera which automatically adjusts itself to changing light conditions.

What about the high cost of vanishing golf balls? You can now purchase a bleeper ball with a self-contained transmitter that sends out radio signals to let you know where it is.

Bulky pocket calculators that take up more room than a pack of cigarettes? Melcor Electronics has a super-mini only half an inch thick, weighing four ounces, and costing just under a hundred dollars.

Bathroom showers which keep fading from hot to cold and back again? Westinghouse has unveiled a "people washer" designed to spray you with soap, rinse you off, and dry you with a blast of hot air. All you have to do is dial the desired temperature and length of time.

("Why can't they make one that dials itself for God's sake? One that reads my mind and shuts itself off when I've had enough?")

Are clothes which require a pressing after only six months of constant wear your particular *bete noir*? A completely wrinkle-free fabric is now available, as well as clothing that changes color with the press of a button, clothing with germicidal fibers to protect you against germs, and, soon to come, clothing with solar-powered temperature coils (microscopic and undetectable of course) to air condition your tender young body in warm weather and heat it in cold—but *exactly*!

What "they" will think of next is impossible to say. Even the above list of exotic luxuries is growing quaint and old-fashioned. The pessimists are predicting that we are doomed to bury ourselves beneath an avalanche of junk. (Where are we going to *throw* it all?) But new products are being constructed of biodegradable glass and plastic which dissolve harmlessly into the environment when we are done with them. Our accelerating technology is providing solutions to anticipated (and present) problems in the course of its own evolution. It is as though the technology is developing a mind of its own—a cybernetic intelligence of sorts—which is telling us: "Don't worry, humans. We've got the whole thing programmed for success." The answers become evident before the questions are asked. Soon the entire law of cause and effect may be reversed. Time itself may be stood on its head as the future is transformed into the present and past. We are being forced to look backward to find out what is happening. History and futurology are blending together and growing indistinguishable. New developments are coming at us at a blinding rate, but we are still living on the same time schedule as our primal ancestors.

There was some resistance to gimmickry such as wall-sized television screens in the beginning. The grim specter of Ray Bradbury's lobotomized human robots glued to their wall screens in *Fahrenheit 451* was still fresh in the public mind. Yet, no sooner did we claim that Gargantuan toy as our own, when we grew bored with it and moved along to something else. Bradbury's mistake (visionary as he was) was in depicting that stage of human development as a static never-changing period. He fell into the same trap we all do from time to time: conjuring an image of some futuristic horror, and then stopping the reel of human history as though we would remain stuck there forever.

Our impatience is our greatest virtue. We can never be satisfied living indefinitely in the present—whatever the present happens to be. Or at least let's hope not. Our notions of progress must be constantly evolving. Stagnation is death even under the best of circumstances.

5

Forgive me if I have been sounding a trifle irritable during the past few pages. Perhaps the reader will be good enough to attribute this to the grumpiness of a writer who grows tired of the battle from time to time, but dares not abandon the battlefield for fear of giving the enemy an unguarded inch. What was it that Jefferson once said about the price of liberty being eternal vigilance? And what price sanity? We are dealing with an opposition that refuses to accept the facts of reality for what they are. If Orwell was right in one regard, it was his projection about the corruption of language into double-think. The Doomsday Brigade has honed this ability to a fine art. If the alarmists cannot convert us through logic, they will subvert the entire reasoning process. I grow edgy, not with the impatience (which I consider virtuous) of an ever-more-demanding consumer, but with the nagging persistance of an enemy camp which refuses to fade away. And so I must remain on guard when I would rather be doing other things—like working on that novel I've been wanting to finish, or taking an extended carefree tour through the Orient. But I cannot, you see. Like Jefferson, I must remain eternally vigilant. Such is the nature of my compulsion, my neurosis. I am a victim of my own optimism, committed to the substantiation of my own scenarios. There is simply too much at stake. I cannot permit the Doomsday Brigade to disseminate its miasmic philosophy with impunity. Such insidious despair ought not to be left unchallenged.

Even while I am writing this, even while the doomsday criers are generating new predictions of collapse and decay, incredible new products are hitting the market daily. The latest homes are coming equipped with liquid crystal windows which turn cloudy or clear upon the turn of a switch. No more shades, curtains, or drapery. We have instant stained glass windows (yes, they come in color) affording maximum privacy as well as beauty upon demand. Electroluminescent threads, developed by the Astronics Corporation, can be woven into the wallpaper and ceilings, eliminating the old-fashioned lightbulb as a source of light. The cost of housing has been vastly reduced by the Conquik House, a one-piece concrete dwelling which can be erected for four thousand dollars. No more high-interest mortgage payments lasting the better part of one's lifetime.

Nor is there any need to worry when one is driving to the seashore about lights or gas ranges left on at home. Remote control switches invented by RCA make it possible to turn appliances on and off from miles away. Vacuum toilets are also standard features in most homes.

They are clean, silent, and never clog up—a bad development for the plumbers but a great benefit to homeowners who used to spend entire weekends wrestling with a mechanical snake and rubber plunger. Automated faucets turn on these days at the mere approach of human skin, while a dial regulates both pressure and temperature. It is also possible to cook a meal in seconds with safe new microwave ovens, locate your children with electronic "radar" screens hooked into the television set, cool or heat your entire house with portable cooling and heating units which can be carried from room to room, burgle-proof your house or apartment with voice-sensitive locks which open only upon a specific voice command, and . . . why bother? It is literally impossible to keep up with it all.

The point is, we are living in a world of unprecedented leisure, surrounded by spellbinding luxuries developed for the multitudes by human genius and ingenuity. It is almost as though every man, woman, and child on earth (certainly within the next ten years this will be the case) had suddenly developed the touch of Midas. Incredible new gadgets are ours, if not for the asking, then only for the outlay of relatively modest sums of money. And yet . . . and yet . . . in the midst of it all: renewed pessimism, additional scenarios of darkness, chaos, and ultimate collapse.

What is doomsday anyway? Someone once sardonically described it as the absence of luxuries our fathers never knew were necessary. Perhaps we have reached that point after all. Is doomsday now to be defined as the breakdown of our vacuum-flush toilets? The shattering of our liquid crystal windows? The theft of our remote-control appliance switches? The malfunction of our newest Patek Philippe watch?

Spoiled children of the new technological era! Have we forgotten how recently (historically speaking) disease and pestilence plagued the earth? How recently filth and squalor were the norm rather than the exception? How recently war and violence were the standard means of birth control? How recently entire homes were lighted with a gas lamp while today planet earth blazes like a Christmas tree? How recently widespread famine sent whole populations scurrying across an ocean in search of fertile land? How recently newborn infants stood less than a fifty-fifty chance of survival? How recently intense cold and heat and other vagaries of weather victimized us all? How recently eternal back-breaking labor was the price we had to pay for a roof above our heads and a loaf of bread at night?

So do not speak to me any more of doomsday projections. Do not speak to me any more of pessimism and despair. Do not speak to me any more of pollution and famine and overpopulation and ecological crises which will bring our civilization crashing around our heads. Do not speak to me any more of man's inherent stupidity and evil and the need for a global dictatorship to mother us all. I have had enough of this sort of twaddle to last me sixteen lifetimes. I have had enough of the Paul Ehrlichs and Barry Commoners and Julian Huxleys and Luther Evanses of the world. They are nagging irrationalists and, worse than that, crushing bores. They have been on stage long enough and it is time they stood aside and gave the rest of us a little peace.

6

After rereading the above, it appears I have grown irritable again. Ah, well. Enough said. The point is made. I have to end this here and hop into my people-washer for a quick scrub. Then it will be time for another antiaging pill (I notice that a hint of gray has seeped back into my hair once more). After that, I will plug myself into the electronic exerciser and vibratone my body to a healthy sheen. Finally, I will snap on my wall screen and watch the evening news. Then let my mind wander away and dream about that novel. I know (I am absolutely certain) I am going to finish it one day soon.

X

Beyond Semi-Literacy

1

In 1976 Albert Shanker held a press conference to denounce the latest trends in education. "The boob tube has taken over the classroom," he said. "If this continues it will mean the end of the teaching profession as we have come to know and love it."

"But, Mr. Shanker," said an eager young newshound from the *New York Post*. "Kids love television. Their reading scores are up, and they're learning to write their names and count their toes for the first time in history."

"It doesn't matter," said Albert Shanker. "Teachers feel more irrelevant and insecure in their own classrooms. Nobody pays attention to us anymore. We're made to feel alienated and unwanted."

"But children are prospering," countered another reporter. "They *like* going to the new Learning Centers, and they had to be dragged to school before."

"What about us?" Shanker yelled. He was visibly perplexed. "What about *our* right to make a decent living? Why should our job security be threatened just so a bunch of lousy kids can learn the alphabet?"

"Easy, Al. Don't overdo it," an aide whispered in his ear.

Shanker pushed him away and continued: "Kids today have no respect for organized labor. They're out to bust our union and we're not gonna let them get away with it. Tomorrow night at midnight every teacher in the country will be walking off the job. Teach the little dummies a lesson."

There was much opposition to Shanker's militant stand among the rank-and-file. Many saw the handwriting on the wall and were afraid of overplaying their hand. But their leader would not be appeased; his mind was made up. At midnight on September 15, 1976, virtually every public school teacher in the United States walked off the job with the intention of teaching the nation's youth a lesson it would never forget. Shanker would have been more prudent had he listened to some of his assistants, for his strategy was destined to fail right from the start. It was the old question of supply and demand all over again. Shanker and his United Teachers Union had the supply—almost every elementary and high school teacher signed up—but the demand for their services was just about nonexistent. Respect for teachers and the product they were offering had been declining for over a decade, and by the time Shanker called his press conference in the year of America's bicentennial the situation had reached a crucial stage. Teachers all over the country were experiencing identity crises, and a good many were spending half their salaries on psychiatrists and other gurus. Shanker and his cohorts had good reason to be miffed. Like alchemists, blacksmiths, gandydancers, woodcarvers, witch doctors, toll collectors, kings, queens, dukes, regents, court jesters, foot soldiers, valets, river boat captains, town criers, pirates, and epic poets, members of the teaching profession saw their own jobs growing obsolete.

Yes, Albert Shanker's strategy backfired; 1976 marks the year that the teachers of America walked off the job and were never asked to return. Once the strike action by the teachers had become permanent (unintentionally), education grew more and more feasible. Great hordes of the nation's youth entered the ranks of the semiliterate for the first time, while countless others dazzled even their own parents with their remarkable erudition.

2

The collapse of public education in the United States of America did not create an educational vacuum by any means. Quite the opposite. Voucher systems were implemented in most states by the late 1970s, and, consequently, private schools grew more competitive. Parents were able to use the vouchers in any school of their choice and, in most cases, they opted for Montessori and other private systems they previously could not afford. Racial integration was also accomplished voluntarily with free-choice education, and people discovered they did not resent members of different races and ethnic backgrounds when they were not rammed down their throats. People picked schools for their children according to their cultural and intellectual tastes, and were therefore drawn together by common standards rather than racial considerations. As a result, social tensions were relaxed for the first time in decades.

By 1980, compulsory education laws were abolished in most states. It had become apparent during the previous few years that adults were as much in need of education as their offspring, and it was manifestly unfair to force children into public schools when their parents were still unable to read a book without getting a migraine headache. So it came to pass that the closed-classroom method of education was abandoned. As more and more people opted for the private schools, public school systems (particularly in the large urban centers) were forced to shut down for good. Existing private schools became more innovative, experimenting with "open classrooms" and "schools without walls," while new groups emerged spontaneously putting even more daring theories into practice. Ivan Illich's concept of "deschooling" society began to take hold in a very real way. With a declining school-age population we did not need as much classroom space as in the past; this, combined with the fact that a static classroom came to be viewed as an obsolete educational environment, made it possible to close down institutional structures which were expensive to build and maintain and convert them into hospitals and apartment buildings. As schools were dismantled or sold off to private bidders, many communities recognized the need for an imaginative alternative to fill the vacuum.

Yes, a new concept of education arose and has pretty well taken hold today. Phase out the old, phase in the new. The Community Learning Center has, for the most part, replaced the foreboding, institutionalized, prison-like public schools of the past.

3

The Community Learning Center. An idea whose time has come. Most neighborhoods and villages have already built one, and those that haven't are in the process of doing so. By and large, they have become extensions of the local library. At one time libraries contained only books and magazines. They were places where one could skim through some periodicals, do research for a book or article or term paper, then check out a few books to read at home. In the late 1960s and early 1970s, many communities expanded these facilities. They stored records and cassettes as well as books and magazines; they put on puppet shows and plays for neighborhood children; showed film classics in the evenings for adults and older students; and invited poets, journalists, novelists, and various dignitaries to read from their work or speak on different subjects to anyone who cared to attend. By the middle-1970s the larger libraries had become a multimedia environment. Print, audiovisuals, electronics, live lectures, and the performing arts coexisted in an atmosphere of dynamic and continuous communication. It soon became obvious that everyone could learn in this kind of a situation. Children, teenagers, young adults, the middle aged, and elderly came together spontaneously, testing their individual ideas, acting and reacting, cross-fertilizing one another intellectually, communicating and interacting in a friendly atmosphere of open-minded curiosity.

Children with the elderly; youth with their parents and the parents of other youth; middle aged and elderly; elderly and college aged; male and female; male and male; female and female; cross-fertilizing; communicating; exchanging and testing ideas; throwing out concepts and absorbing new ones; dynamic; spontaneous; print and audiovisual; electronic and vocal; educational; electrifying; open-minded; stimulating; action and reaction; respect; toleration; understanding; civilized and dynamic; communication and education.

The library (soon to be called the Community Learning Center) became the focal point of one's neighborhood or community. More and more people gravitated there spontaneously. People of all ages and interests. They learned the alphabet, learned to count and read and write, listened to lectures and music, taught one another, planned field trips, visited museums and other communities. The elderly no longer felt isolated from society. The young had much to learn from them and they, in turn, were able to stay abreast of new developments and ideas. In effect, everyone became a teacher and a student simultaneously.

Even higher levels of education have been similarly affected. No longer do we pay dull, pedantic "professors" eighteen and twenty thousand dollars a year to drone away in front of a classroom for six or eight hours a week, and publish (or perish!) an obscure paper once a year which only fourteen people will attempt to read and half of them be unable to finish. Today, a group of students hire an expert in a particular field—engineering, physics, biochemistry, writing, literature, whatever—to tutor them for a fee over a fixed period. When they have picked his brain and learned everything he has to teach them, they move on to someone else. Education is more effective and much less expensive this way. Students benefit from the knowledge and experience of an individual who is a *working member of his profession* rather than a full-time academician with no experience or proven ability in his area of alleged expertise. It makes far greater sense to have successful writers teach others how to write, and successful scientists teach the basics of thermonuclear fusion, rather than grant tenure to someone whose knowledge is purely theoretical.

Yes, the concept has fully caught on. Community Learning Centers are here to stay (until we discover an even better method of educating and learning). Communication and education are now synonymous. Education, once a static, inefficient, one-dimensional system with "teacher" funneling information to "student," is a dynamic and continuous life experience.

4

Thanks to cable television and modern cassettes, most homes today provide something more of an educational atmosphere than in the past. Cable television was allowed to flourish unmolested after a brief period of government interference in the early and middle-

1970s. Thanks to the climate of freedom in this field, the United States developed a totally free electronic communication system for the first time.

In the days prior to cable television there were only a few networks in the country, all of which were licensed and regulated by the federal government. As a result, programming was insipid and lacked daring for the most part; even news coverage tended to be bland and conformist, reflecting an established bias with little room provided for originality of thought. Newscasters themselves were all hammered out of the same mold. They projected the image of the Compleat Bloomingdale Man, from the cut of their suits to the shape of their hairstyles (hair*cuts* were passé by the end of the 1960s) to their broad toothy smiles to the Finishing School cosmopolite accent. Yes, the networks pretended to be competitive, pretended to serve the primary media function of an additional check on surging political power and corruption, pretended to be free, open-ended, spontaneous, creative, energetic, and democratic, but were instead timid, rigid, self-righteous, narrow-minded, and totalitarian in both attitude and taste. The American television networks were more effective than the nationalized media in Europe and elsewhere, to be sure, but were still a far way off from fulfilling the original promise of the First Amendment to the United States Constitution.

By 1976 most Americans had grown thoroughly disgusted with watching the same pap and drivel night after night on their television sets. Consequently, electronic games emerged as the most popular pastime in the country. Instead of turning on the TV to Dick Van Dyke or the evening news, millions of viewers hooked electronic tennis, ping pong, and football games into their sets for a night's entertainment. Media executives were fired by the dozens. Many Americans suffered severe withdrawal symptoms—ticks, stuttering, nervous giggles—in making the transition to do-it-yourself amusement, but these were shortlived. By 1977 the major concern of the television industry was: how to lure more than two hundred and ten millions of Americans back to the tube.

Then cable television blossomed and changed all that. Cable technology made it possible for the viewer to receive dozens, even hundreds, of new programs on his home television set. In addition, the public was paying for the cost through subscription fees which meant that private censorship, in the form of sponsor-control of content, was automatically eliminated. A great variety of programs offering every shade of political view and cultural taste was suddenly available to the viewing public. By the late 1970s competition, not only among the various cable companies, but among ideas, styles, and standards was a reality in America for the first time. It is interesting (as well as refreshing) to see which have survived and which have fallen by the wayside during the past few years. Educational programs, particularly, have become a great hit with families all over the country. Children learn the rudiments of language and math, while parents take college-level courses at home and complete educations they previously had to abandon until much later in their lives. Courses of study also come preprogrammed in cassettes which are plugged into the home TV set.

(On Oceana I, the first residential Disneyland erected in the mid-Atlantic, a novel approach has proved extremely successful. Disney characters are trotted out in educational cartoons to teach the kiddies their lessons. Youngsters are studying at the feet of Donald Duck, Elmer Fudd, Mickey Mouse, Bugs Bunny, Pluto, and other comic strip characters. The cute little devils can't wait to line up in front of the tube each day to learn their ABCs.)

5

The educational process is also enhanced by technology

and the ease with which one can travel these days. In the past provincialism was virtually synonymous with ignorance, and the most dangerous thing about ignorance is that it is contagious. It breeds fear, suspicion, and pettiness which usually erupt into galloping paranoia and violence. As long as this infectious condition existed, the ideal of a peaceful and civilized world could only remain a distant dream. How could one fight provincialism, isolation, and ignorance? Not by abandoning technology and returning to the past. And certainly not by turning the earth into a global village, notwithstanding the sometimes-worthy exhortations of McLuhan, Fuller, and others. Herman Kahn was more on target when he spoke in terms of a global *metropolis*. Historically, it was in the cities where the civilized life has flourished, where the pristine hillbilly was transformed into a tolerant, urbane, and sophisticated citizen. It was in the cities where provincialism and ignorance were beaten down and drummed out of existence, where music, literature, art, civility—all the worthwhile things of life—found their voice, came into their own, and were rendered into magic. Yes, it was only by making the earth a world metropolis, a universal seedbed of the civilized life, that ignorance could be destroyed and the truly educated society could come into existence.

The cement that has always held the city together, that gave it status and identity, was the technology of communication. As this technology evolved from hand-scrawled, hand-delivered letters to the printing press, the telephone, the telegraph, radio and television, and then to global satellites, the cities also grew up, grew more efficient and sophisticated, and finally reached a point where they were ready to burst through their boundaries, explode and self-destruct with uncontrollable energy.

They could no longer be contained but rather needed room to expand and flesh out the universe.

So we developed the technology to create our global metropolis and obliterate provincialism. (Perhaps paradoxically, there are more open spaces today and more parks and greenery than in the past. The world metropolis I am speaking of is a universal communication network, not a pile of flesh and blood and glass and concrete structures. The world metropolis, you see, is a state of mind and a condition of life—not a geographical center. It is a dynamic combine of ideas and energy and, as such, has little to do with the physical cities that grew up over the centuries because of economic realities.) For something like three or four dollars on weekends and weekday nights, a farmer in South Dakota can pick up his telephone and contact his counterpart in Samoa, Mozambique, and the Australian outback. There is still a language barrier, to be sure, and will be for some time yet, but at least the physical barriers isolating one community from another (the westside of Manhattan from Flemington, New Jersey, for that matter) have been overcome.

These relatively inexpensive round-the-world telephone calls are possible only if the telephones are working in the first place. At one time vandalism had transmogrified most of our public telephone booths—especially in the larger cities—into little more than urban outhouses, but Mother Bell developed a system to change all that. Today we carry small portable telephones around with us. The phones are activated when we step inside circular electromagnetic fields built by the telephone company, and the calls are billed to credit cards or our home telephone numbers.

Also available today are cassette telephones for sending messages to many people simultaneously; self-dialing telephones that respond to a voice command; wristwatch telephones which will bring us another step beyond the Dick Tracy two-way wrist radio; home sentinel telephones which inform us of fires, burglaries, and other extraordinary occurrences while we are away; picture phones (the more advanced models supply printed pictures of the screen image); credit phones allowing the caller to order merchandise and pay bills without leaving bed; and the list grows longer and longer even as we pause a moment to catch our breath. What all this translates into is the fact that instantaneous communication grows more and more commonplace among individuals as well as corporations. Provincial barriers and attitudes are broken down as the world becomes a single, dynamic, interrelating community. Words such as *foreign*, *alien*, *strange*, *different*, and *enemy* are losing their meanings as we become citizens of the same free world society (as distinct from a static global dictatorship).

Despite the dire predictions of Marshall McLuhan fifteen years ago, the printed word is playing an even more important role then it did in the past. The book publishing industry has been modernized and wrenched out of the nineteenth century where it wallowed for a hundred and seventy-odd years. Through microfiching, more than a hundred books are imposed on a four-by-six inch plastic card. Instead of visiting mammoth bookstores with sturdy volumes toppling off the shelves—bookstores incapable of storing the fifty thousand books published in the United States alone each year—we go to microfiching libraries where an almost unlimited supply of printed words are stored in incredibly small areas. You order the book of your choice and computerized machines print it out and bind it for you in minutes. This saves the publisher a boodle in production costs since he no longer has to manufacture and distribute thousands of books beforehand (and worry about remainders afterward), and it relieves the bookseller of the guesswork regarding which books should be ordered and kept in stock.

(The only casualties under this system are the authors themselves, who used to glory at the sight of their books prominently displayed near the cash register when they walked into Brentano's. Perhaps advertising posters will provide the same balm for ruptured egos.)

Superphones and instant books. What else does our global cosmopolis have to offer? Electronic newspapers are now the order of the day. Gone forever is the sweaty romanticism of the Runyonesque reporter, his filthy fedora jauntily angled on the back of his head, the constant cigarette working in the corner of his mouth as he tapped out an exclusive on a typewriter built during the early years of the Middle Ages. Yes, Jimmy Breslin was one of the last of a dying breed while the Tom Wolfes of the profession neatly made the transition into the razzle-dazzle kaleidoscopic present. Video typewriters transmit news stories directly to production centers via computerized phototypesetting equipment. Features written and edited electronically are transformed into newsprint without once having been touched by human hands. The whole industry was streamlined beyond recognition as newsrooms lost their cluttered hustle-bustle atmosphere.

(Ah, nostalgia! You prick the psyche with memories. You fill the past with romanticized notions about the good old days. You distort reality. To hell with nostalgia!)

For I, too, benefit from a world of microfiching, computerization, and talking textbooks. How much more comfortable it is doing research at home by dialing the local Learning Center and having a computer read selected pages of books and magazines. No more overflowing metal file cabinets which threatened to take over the apartment.

6

Instant communication. And the transportation of people with their ideas, if not instantaneously then as close to it as possible, to the farthest regions of the earth. It is all well and good for the residents of Asbury Park to know what is happening at this moment to the citizens of Peking. But carrying this concept to its logical conclusion means putting them together in the same room over a bottle of bourbon or a cup of tea. At a price they can afford. Let them gaze upon each other face to face. Somehow foreigners don't seem so menacing when you're staring at their warts and varicose veins. Slants, wops, spades, and spics are suddenly metamorphosed into individuals—short, tall, fat, thin, stupid, and brilliant individuals—with all their kinky foibles reducing them to our own size.

With this goal in mind, rocket planes are being targeted for the late 1980s. By then, if all proceeds according to plan, it will be possible to board a plane in Texas and land in Tokyo a couple of hours later. En route the traveler will be projected into a brief orbit around the earth, experiencing temporary weightlessness, and will reenter the atmosphere for a quick descent to the other side of the planet.

In the meantime, more conventional air travel has been streamlined by computers which coordinate air traffic and relieve the pilot of many decisions regarding change in direction and altitude. Computers permit pilots to fly in poorer weather by analyzing information from the various gauges and making appropriate adjustments. Goodyear Aerospace Corporation has developed a computer to reduce the chances of a midair collision. Staran IV makes forty million calculations a second, and warns air traffic controllers about aircraft headed on a collision course in time for them to do something about it. In Briarcliff Manor, New York, a computer center confirms airline reservations anywhere in the United States, Canada, and Mexico within seconds.

In effect, the entire globe has become a classroom. Ideas move across national borders at the speed of light; people leave home and descend into strange lands from the stratosphere in a matter of hours. The exchange of information and the interrelation of human beings has given new meaning to the concept of education. Education is communication; it is travel; it is understanding and toleration; it is people mixing, moving, criss-crossing the planet at breathtaking speeds, broadening their circle of friends and acquaintances; education is dynamic, continuous, never-ending. Ironically, this accelerated interchange of people and ideas has given birth to a new kind of stability. Knowledge breeds understanding and relaxation of tension. Our society is fluid and, to a great extent, transient; concomitantly, it is relaxed and at peace with itself. Paradox is somewhat deceptive. Perhaps there is truth in contradiction after all.

XI

The Fountain of Youth and Health

1

In another area, the worst fears of Julian Huxley have been realized: sickness and disease are no longer cutting mankind down with the same dispatch they did twenty years ago. People are just not dying off as rapidly as they used to. Huxley is especially fond of the good old days when the infant mortality rate claimed three out of every five newborn children, when the average American lifespan was thirty-five instead of seventy-eight (and rising dramatically), when pneumonia and tuberculosis destroyed an otherwise vigorous individual in the prime of life. Man, "the cancer of the planet," was not quite so arrogant way back then; he was constantly being reminded of his mortality and physical vulnerability; he knelt humbly before the overwhelming power of nature; he did not infest the planet with his strutting omnipresence.

Today the story is different. The last known incidence of smallpox occurred in Pakistan early in 1976. Since then the disease has apparently been obliterated from planet earth. In the early 1970s heart disease was the leading cause of death in the United States, accounting for over one-third of the nearly two million deaths in 1971 alone. Cancer came in second, dispatching people at roughly half the rate of heart disease. By the end of the decade these two major killers were rendered as docile as the common cold (which, ironically, lingers on as one of the most persistent nuisances known to man; aspirin and vitamin C are still touted as the only effective antidotes).

The reason for the demise of the primary natural enemy of man was not so clear in the beginning. The conquest of cancer was more cut-and-dry, attributable as it was to the drugs which produced antibodies to the cancer viruses. Heart disease was a greater mystery, however. Studies released in 1973 revealed that heart disease in the United States was declining, but no one seemed to know exactly why. Was it diet? Better lifestyles? Less drinking and smoking? More exercise? Dr. Peter L. Frommer, the head of the cardiology unit at the National Heart and Lung Institute, admitted that the decline was real but the reason for it was pure guesswork.

Less smoking? Cigarette sales had increased steadily over the years despite the best efforts of the federal government to diminish the tobacco industry.

Less drinking? Cirrhosis of the liver was one of the few diseases (along with bronchitis, emphysema, and asthma) to have increased since the end of World War II. So much for the booze factor.

Better diet? Much-publicized changes in the American diet, away from fat and carbohydrates toward lean meat and natural foods, did not take root on a broad scale until the late 1960s—too late to have affected the charts.

More exercise? Possibly, because Americans had started jogging and burning up the tennis courts in the early 1960s, ten years before the figures were released.

Reduction in stress and tension? If so, this factor was at variance with claims made by the psychological profession to the effect that Americans were literally worrying themselves into early graves.

There were simply too many variables at work for anyone to give a definitive answer to the question. It could have been any one reason alone, or combination of known reasons and others yet undiscovered. Complicating the dilemma even further was the fact that, not just heart disease, but as many as nine of the leading killer diseases affecting man were also on the decline. These included, in addition to heart disease and cancer; strokes and related diseases; the kidney ailments nephritis and nephrosis; peptic ulcers (another indication that a decrease in stress was probably an important factor); arteriosclerosis; birth defects and infant mortality; accidents (which were included among diseases for some reason; mental disease may have had something to do with driving habits); influenza and pneumonia. Some of these declines could be credited to the discovery of new drugs and medicines—penicillin in the case of pneumonia for example—but a decreasing incidence of peptic ulcers and perhaps even arteriosclerosis pointed toward a change in lifestyle and a resulting reduction of tension in daily living as a possible influence. The psychosomatic element suddenly assumed greater importance. Perhaps we were paying too much attention to external symptoms, and not enough to the inner workings of the psyche. Could it be that, deep down in the nether recesses of the human soul, we could discover the root cause of most of our physical ailments?

2

This possibility received considerable support in a study conducted by Dr. Thomas H. Holmes of the University of Washington School of Medicine. Dr. Holmes and others working in the field made the charge (which was understandably unpopular among their colleagues in the AMA) that emotional stress may have been the underlying cause behind many physical ailments—perhaps even most of them. That accursed word, *psychosomatic*, was being resurrected again, this time with an undercoating of scientific data to give it more durability. Research conducted by Dr. Holmes and his staff indicated that widows and widowers died at a rate *ten times greater* during the first year of bereavement than others in their age group; divorced people suffered from illness at twelve times the normal rate for married people in the first year following divorce; and as much as 80 percent of serious physical ailments seemed to occur during periods when the individual was most depressed and psychologically vulnerable. Dr. David Mechanic, a sociologist at the University of Wisconsin, corroborated these findings in an interview published in 1973: "When people are in trouble, they should be given supportive care, not just treated for their physical symptoms and handed a prescription," he said. "Unfortunately, those people who most need an examination of their underlying life situations tend to see doctors in very busy practices where they are least likely to get it."

Operating on the basic theory that emotional tension was the root cause of most physical (and mental) illness, Dr. Holmes devised a system for measuring life-stress situations as scientifically as possible. With the benefit of the ten years' hindsight, Holmes' system appears crude and antediluvian today. But in the context of his time, considering the inchoate nature of the discipline he was developing, his chart was somewhat ingenious and had extremely valuable practical benefits. On a scale of 100, Dr. Holmes rated various situations according to their probable emotional impact on the individual. Topping the list with an impact rating of 100 was the death of a mate. Coming in a rather distant second was divorce, with a 73 rating. Marriage ranked seventh on the chart with a score of 50 (pleasant as well as unpleasant events affected health, said Dr. Holmes, since any abrupt change in daily routine resulted in emotional tension). Other occurrences ranked on the chart included: retirement (45); sex difficulties (39); death of a close friend (37); foreclosure of a mortgage or loan (30); in-law trouble (29); change in residence (20); believe it or not, a vacation (13); and Christmas (12). One's initial reaction, after studying the list, is sheer wonderment over the situations Dr. Holmes might have included but chose to leave out. Wouldn't it have been just as valid to rank, for example, rainy Mondays, overcooked eggs, pens that run out of ink, broken shoelaces, pop-top cans when the poppers snap off, overheated car engines, blown fuses with no replacements in the house, ditto electric lightbulbs (in the few quaint old places where they are still used), and typewriter ribbons which begin typing a pale gray after you have run out in the rain and visited four stationery stores before finding one with the proper ribbon in stock? This last event, it seems to me, deserves a rating somewhere between divorce and marriage at the least, and possibly higher.

But, admittedly, it is nit-picking to demand perfection this way. Holmes was a heroic pioneer in a field demanding daring exploration, and he deserves better treatment. (I am writing this on a rainy Saturday with a defective typewriter ribbon after overcooking my poached eggs; my emotional impact quotient has already shot through the roof and I feel a case of bubonic plague coming on.) Additional research by Holmes and others revealed that a clustering of events within a short period often precedes the onslaught of diseases ranging from heart attacks to ulcers and mental disturbances. Holmes and his colleagues started looking for traumatic experiences in the lives of patients, and they were able to draw a direct corollary between the relative emotional tension and the seriousness of the illness. The likelihood of disease increased proportionately to the impact of life-stress experiences. The studies further indicated that an accumulation of 200 or more impact units in a single year was more than most people could handle. The recommended therapy? Take it easy for a while, rest, relax, and consult with a physician or counselor if necessary. If an individual had already built up a stockpile of tension units, he should wait before embarking on disruptive new experiences such as buying or selling a house, changing jobs, and so on. The idea was, *not* to become a vegetable, but rather to maintain the routine and avoid abrupt alterations in lifestyle until stored-up tension had been allowed to dissipate somewhat.

A variation on this theme was proposed by another researcher in the field, Dr. Lawrence E. Hinkle, Jr., of the Division of Human Ecology (how's that for a division?) at Cornell University Medical School. Hinkle suggested that it was not the experiences themselves that brought on sickness and disease, but the way each individual handled them. He took issue with Dr. Holmes' practice of ascribing an absolute rating to each event since one individual might fall apart at the prospect of losing his job, while a more self-controlled person could withstand a divorce, the death of a relative, and financial difficulties without breaking stride. The problem, said Hinkle, was how to cope with disruptive situations when they occurred rather than avoiding them (which might be impossible in any case). A lively debate ensued over whether or not Dr. Hinkle was advocating that people turn themselves into "emotional monsters," with shallow attachments to other individuals and groups. The questions were valid. Was someone who could easily shift his allegiance to a new partner following a divorce an unfeeling monster, or a strong individual with an instinct for survival? How about the person who was adept at steeling himself against the emotional impact of a friend's death? Was it better to give in to grief and *feel* experiences to the marrow, or shore up the emotions against the impact of tension which could lead to sickness? Or was there a happy medium in the case of someone who reacted emotionally to events, yet was controlled enough to keep them from damaging his physical and mental equilibrium?

Exciting and provocative questions, to be sure. They were brand new and seemingly insoluble in 1974. Today, ten years later, we know much more about the human psyche. We know more about how it works and how the individual can control the most subtle influences on his biochemical makeup through mind power. Mind control is now an exact, measurable science. Through it we have eliminated sickness and disease. Fairly soon, we may conquer the most tyrannical of all diseases known to man: the aging process itself.

3

Biofeedback. Mind control. Self-mastery over the mind and body. A science fiction concept a short while ago. Today an exact science, an infant discipline which is opening great new horizons for the human potential. Biofeedback techniques were first developed in the early 1970s at the Menninger Foundation in Topeka, Kansas. Dr. Elmer E. Green, the foundation director at the time, trained people to regulate their blood pressure, temperature, and other biological functions through sheer willpower. He evolved the theory that everyone could learn to recognize emotional stress as it occurred and, by transmitting brain waves to selected areas of the body, ward off heart disease, peptic ulcers, migraine headaches, hypertension, asthma, insomnia, hardening of the arteries, depression, and other ailments. Imbalances in our physiological structure could be corrected before they did any damage. Dr. Green went on to claim that as much as 80 percent of all illness was at least partially psychosomatic, usually originating in tension brought on by emotional strain. In brief, proper mental attitudes (scientifically measured with biofeedback machines) could alter body chemistry and keep us young and healthy.

This was revolutionary stuff at the time, and was initially dismissed as pseudomystical rubbish in the same category as psychokinesis and other occult fads. But Dr. Green and the foundation he served carried reputable credentials and were not so easily put off. He substantiated his findings with hard facts and established biofeedback as an important (perhaps the most important) preventive medicine technique within a few short years. Today, most homes are considered unfinished without at least one biofeedback machine on the premises; many boast individual units for each member of the family.

Another theory developed during this period, apparently as a natural adjunct to the advances being made in biofeedback, was the definition of aging as just one more disease yet to be conquered by man. What did we know about aging anyway? We recognized various physical characteristics as they occurred. After a certain stage in life the hair turned progressively grayer and usually thinned out; the skin began to wrinkle and sag; eyesight dimmed like fading headlights when the battery runs down; the joints tended to stiffen and swell; the muscles shrunk and refused to perform as reliably as they used to; hearing was not so acute as in the past. Internally, we were able to measure additional changes. Brain cells died off and affected memory and other mental faculties; the heart pumped blood more slowly; lungs took in decreasing amounts of oxygen; the kidneys grew less proficient; bladder control diminished; hormone output dwindled.

Yes, we knew all too well the demoralizing symptoms of aging. For centuries we did our best to hide them in every way possible. We turned to wigs, cosmetics, girdles, facelifts, and more recently to hair transplants and specious hormone treatments for the skin. At best, all these were nothing but holding actions. They covered the symptoms, improved our frame of mind a bit, camouflaged a worsening situation more to ourselves than to others. The inexorable devastation of our bodies continued on schedule, and we slapped a little plaster here and there, a little paint somewhere else, hoping against hope that no one else would notice the gradual deterioration. Like restored old tenements we offered a sunny face to the viewing public, but inside the plumbing was decaying and the joints were coming undone.

We understood the *what* of aging, but not the *why*. Why did it have to happen in the first place? Was there some divine law which stated that an individual had to fall apart in stages as he wended his way through life? At one time a few among us believed it was unnatural to fly since we did not have wings, yet we built our own wings and took to the air anyway. If *unnatural* was synonymous with *immoral*, then the human race would be condemned to live at the mercy of the elements until the end of time. For what are glass and concrete houses, automobiles, air conditioners, and heating units if not unnatural? No, the old arguments against tampering with the natural processes simply would not hold up.

The questions persisted: Why did we age? And could anything be done about it? Was not a species capable of mastering the law of gravity and reaching toward the stars also capable of attending to his own archaic genetic technology? None but the surliest pessimists would doubt it.

4

Once aging was accepted as another disease, the next step was to go out and find a cure for it. In the early 1970s we began to make some headway in this direction. Various researchers, some working independently and others in close communication with their colleagues, started to unravel the mysteries of the aging process and issued statements that we would soon learn how to slow it down, and eventually reverse it. Doctors and biochemists in the United States and Europe held out the promise of extended youth and vigor for mankind, and dramatically increased lifespans in the foreseeable future. In 1973 Dr. Alex Comfort, director of gerontology research at University College in London, stated: "We hope to find a technique for interfering with human aging within the next four or five years—not for stopping the process, but for slowing it down."

Others in the field, including Dr. Bernard Strehler of the University of Southern California, were even more optimistic. Strehler claimed that human beings "may live almost indefinitely" some day. Reputable biochemists were suddenly predicting average human lifespans of ninety to a hundred and twenty by the end of the century. These were not charlatans or headline-grabbers, but leading members of a profession which has tended to be conservative and extremely cautious. Dr. Nathan W. Shock, the chief of Baltimore's Gerontology Research Center of the National Institute of Child Health and Human Development (NICHHD) in the early and middle 1970s, one of the more conservative people in the field, admitted that substantial breakthroughs in anti-aging techniques were being achieved. "The more we know about the underlying causes of aging," said Shock, "the more we are apt to be able to devise and introduce a drug or pill or experimental condition that can have an impact." There was no simple cause of aging, but the possible causes had been narrowed to an identifiable few, all of which could be controlled with further research.

The major factor in the view of most biochemists was heredity. This theory held that all living creatures are born with an "inner clock" which is programmed to run out after a set period of time. Hence, assuming that all diseases and accidental causes of death could be eliminated, man was programmed by nature to expire after a maximum lifespan of a hundred and ten years or thereabouts. His biological system would simply wind down and cease functioning. But this process need not be inevitable. Dr. Leonard Hayflick, a gentleman who has spent most of his life doing research on human cells, stated that drugs could be created which would control the rejuvenation of cells and keep them from expiring. In effect, the drugs would continually wind up the inner clock so that it need never run down.

Other biochemists concentrated on different aspects of aging, including: hormonal changes in the body; chemical alteration of the brain cells; derangement of the immune system; destructive free-radical and cross-linkage agents; and several closely related phenomena. By 1974 the researchers announced progress on all fronts. Drugs were devised to correct hormone imbalances and reverse senile dementia or the impairment of brain activities. Damaged immune systems would soon be repaired by the injection of bacteria. And the free-radical and cross-linkage agents in the body could be neutralized by antioxidant chemicals, including Vitamin E in combination with other elements. A drug called Procaine or Gerovital H-3, developed by Dr. Ana Aslan of Rumania, went on sale in England, Switzerland, and West Germany in the early 1970s. The FDA banned its sale in the United States at first, but when reports of its limited success emanated from Europe, it was finally allowed on the American market by the middle of 1976. Gerovital was effective in reversing wrinkling of the skin and graying of the hair to some extent, but no one claimed it was a panacea for all our aging problems. It was, however, the first known product producing any beneficial results at all, and as such a major advance in the field.

Ironic, isn't it, that the long-sought-after Fountain of Youth appeared to be materializing in the form of yet one more pill?

5

With all this going on, the science of biofeedback was unlocking the secrets of another aspect of aging. Mental attitudes and psychological factors were also at work. Investigators at the Menninger Foundation, Duke University, and other notable institutions discovered that an individual's personal psychology was extremely influential in determining how well he would do in later life. A "high happiness" rating, said Dr. Erdman Palmore of Duke, coincided with a long and vigorous life. "Remaining active in some meaningful role affected people's longevity on all three major levels—physical, psychological, and social." A lot had to do with a person's attitude toward growing old. The ones who survived longest and remained productive were those refusing to throw in the towel. They exercised their bodies and minds, remarried when widowed, kept working or took up a fulfilling hobby, walked, read, and did not worry too much about aging. Those who *believed* they would fall apart, and agonized constantly about it, did so. Life and what one made of it was by-and-large a self-fulfilling prophecy. If one anticipated senility he would bring it on more rapidly. Biofeedback taught people to control their physical nature to a great extent through mind control. Within the past few years we have learned to reverse hardening of the arteries with the help of our biofeedback machines. Extremists in this field make the assertion that *all* symptoms of aging can be corrected by biofeedback. More cautious types like myself prefer to use it in conjunction with antiaging pills. Everyone to his own remedy. I don't begrudge the pharmaceutical companies their handsome profits if they are doing the job. If others think the new pills are a "capitalist rip-off," let them meditate with their machines to their hearts' content. It's all the same to me.

Many people were concerned about the social consequences of life extension when the first breakthroughs were made. The average American today lives thirty-one years longer than he did at the turn of the century. How would this affect the social and economic structure of the country? What about pensions and social security payments that have to be paid for longer periods? What about mandatory retirement at age sixty-five for an individual who is still in his prime? Wouldn't this result in alienation, depression, and possibly suicide? How about overpopulation (that old bugaboo again) with selfish old fogeys refusing to kick the bucket when they're supposed to? The Doomsday Brigade had a proverbial field day in the summer and fall of 1976 over these little items. The call went out for a "moratorium on antiaging research" pending a United Nations study on the "social, economic, and ecological consequences" of extended youth and vitality. Julian Huxley thought we should find a drug to "*accelerate* the aging process" so people would die off even faster than usual. Susan Sontag modified this proposal to "premature senility for white people only," the real problem on planet earth according to her, while Paul Ehrlich qualified it yet further to "mandatory senility for white Americans living west of the Hudson River and east of the Continental Divide."

Margaret Mead had no comment on Ehrlich's suggestion.

James Reston thought it a "bit extreme."

Max Lerner claimed it was a "modest proposal."

Paul Kurtz regarded Ehrlich as a "horse's ass for not including urban blacks, chicanos, and other superfluous groups."

William Buckley said Ehrlich himself was already "prematurely senile, incorrectably so."

For the first time in ten years I found myself agreeing with Bill Buckley.

Luther Evans called for the creation of a World Senility Board which would determine just who should be given senility pills, and who would be allowed to remain young as long as possible.

After considerable soul-searching, John Lindsay cast his lot with the Huxley-Ehrlich-Evans axis, claiming their position was the "most humanitarian one yet devised by a human brain." (It was learned later that Lindsay had already purchased a ten-year supply of Gerovital, and his statement was somewhat discredited.)

Tom Wicker wrote an article maintaining that Lindsay's hypocrisy was not sufficient grounds for sullying his image as "the most humane political candidate yet conjured by any political party, left, right, or in betwixt."

Germaine Greer wrote a best-selling book called *Dirty Old Men I Have Known and Loved*. In it she detailed her fondness for beer-drinking, cigar-chomping, foul-mouthed veterans of the coal mines and the construction trades. "I have always found rank old goats more sexually stimulating than young pretty boys," said she.

All in all it was one hell of a debate, and it diverted the nation's attention from a rather tedious presidential election that year.

6

The worst fears concerning the social consequences of extended youth and life were all in vain, however. When Social Security was made voluntary in 1977, most American wage earners decided to switch to private retirement programs. Consequently, American taxpayers will not have to worry about carrying the burden of endless payments to long-living individuals in the future. Mandatory retirement laws were almost completely abolished by 1979, and most Americans in their seventies and eighties today work part-time to supplement incomes from private pensions and Social Security (in the case of those who were forced into the system throughout most of their lives). Overpopulation is not a problem since the birthrate is declining dramatically almost everywhere on earth, and no pill yet invented (alas!) can prevent someone from losing his life in a serious accident. Within thirty years, though, we will be able to reconstruct an individual genetically from a single living cell. Even his memory bank will be rebuilt in the laboratory, certifying that the remade human is actually the original and not just a look-alike clone. (I have developed an almost pathological fear of risking my life in any way until this type of genetic restructuring has become a reality.)

A decade ago there was a good deal of worry that the emerging antiaging technology could also lead to abuses, particularly in the areas of behavior modification through drugs, psychosurgery, manipulation of the genes, and pacemakers or monitors implanted in the brain. These were serious concerns for decent people all over the political scale. Happily, legislation was passed in 1977 prohibiting the "*involuntary* alteration of any individual's behavior patterns," and "the adulteration of genes in a fetus for any purpose other than correcting mental and/or physical birth defects." Hence, genetic engineering is used today strictly for beneficial purposes—to assure newborn children of a life as healthy, functioning human beings, and our technology is used to modify criminal tendencies at the request of prisoners who would otherwise be incarcerated indefinitely for their crimes. The legislation has also outlawed the proposals of people like B. F. Skinner and other behaviorists, who would alter the behavior patterns of newborn infants to suit their own political ideologies. No such experimentation can be practiced legally today, and most people are breathing more easily for it. All attempts to change the basic nature of human beings while they are still gestating in the womb, or through controlled environments later on, are no longer permissible (if, indeed, it is possible to do so in the first place). The role of guinea pig has been relegated to the lower animals—until such a time, at least, as they begin picketing for their own rights.

(Will the next wave of student revolutionaries be directed by dolphins? Merry thought, that one.)

7

As I observe the world of 1984, both in my travels and through the electronic eye which scans the entire globe, I see men and women in their seventies and eighties who appear to be contemporaries of their own children. Biologically speaking, we are all contemporaries, although there is no substitute for chronological age as far as experience and knowledge are concerned. The longer we live, the more we learn, understand, and accumulate experiences, and this will always be so. But, physically, chronology is far less important than it used to be, and within the next decade it will become fully obsolete. That well-conditioned woman you see darting around the tennis court, her legs and arms firm, her body trim, her hair lush and full of color, her face smooth and eyes bright, might be thirty-five or fifty or possibly over sixty. You will have to speak to her to determine how long she has actually been alive. That gentleman with the red beard and alert eyes behind the wheel of his car could be seventy or forty-five. It doesn't really matter which; he feels well and performs his job as adroitly as he did thirty years ago. That opera singer you've enjoyed listening to, or the author whose last book made you laugh so much, might have been a doctor for thirty years before turning to the arts. More people launch multiple careers today. After all, it gets boring doing the same thing for such long periods of time; it makes more sense to collect a pension in one field, then move on to an alternate career that would have remained an unfulfilled ambition in the past.

Our antiaging technology has produced other techniques, in addition to biofeedback and the pills, for hanging on to our youth and good health. Experiments conducted more than ten years ago showed that both hibernation and the reduction of body temperature had rejuvenating effects on animals. Dogs, fish, rodents, and other mindless creatures enjoyed longer lifespans under these conditions. The question arose: would human beings be similarly affected?

Additional research provided an affirmative answer. It did not take long for shrewd entrepreneurs the world over to realize the potential in this situation. By 1978 the first hibernation centers were being erected throughout Europe and the American Southwest. Today we have a network extending across the planet. Where only the rich could afford the treatment five short years ago, now most middle-class people find it within their means to hibernate in a low-temperature environment for two or three weeks each year. Those who have done it swear by the experience. They have thrown away their ornamental camouflage—their wigs and face creams—as hibernation regenerates their vital processes.

Diet, too, has been found to play a big role in aging. Not the organic and natural food fads that passed for science in the late sixties and early seventies. Much of that was actually harmful since we later learned that many food additives, particularly chemical antioxidants, had been healthful in ways we never realized. The major breakthrough in this field was the discovery that reduced food intake had a substantial effect on the human lifespan (lifespan of all creatures for that matter). Better health and longer life resulted from small portions of a well-balanced meal. By 1980 it was possible to buy food with anti-aging additives at the local supermarket, and there was a mad rush away from the less nutritious natural foods toward the adulterated stuff. There are still a few diehards who refuse to give up their organic gardens and hope to live forever on a diet of nuts, fruits, and vegetables. But the readership of *Prevention* magazine has fallen off drastically, and the ranks of the "health food" addicts have been badly decimated. It is wise to eat everything, just so long as you do not stuff yourself at each sitting, and the food is amply laced with the proper chemicals.

What else? The age of the cyborg is also upon us. Most of us today have some mechanical parts in our bodies, ranging from contact lenses and hearing aids to the more complicated machinery of artificial hearts, lungs, and kidneys. Cyborg technology has given humanity a lease on life it never dreamed was possible a generation back. Defective body organs need not be a cause of death any longer. In the past, an otherwise healthy person could develop kidney ailments, for example, which affected other parts of the body as they grew more serious. There was a biochemical "domino effect" at work. By the early 1970s we learned to replace defective hearts with transplants from other bodies. A few years later mechanical parts were found to be superior. There was no rejection factor, and the man-made hardware was far more durable. Today the insertion of artificial organs in the human body is a fairly routine procedure. Within four or five years we will be able to rebuild virtually the entire body with hardware, and before the century is out a few among us will be strutting about with artificial brains in their skulls. Automobile and television repairmen are taking night courses in human surgery, a natural transition for them in the age of cyborg technology.

(Amusingly enough, Hubert Humphrey, making his quadrennial stab at the presidency, recently advocated legislation prohibiting marriages between cyborgs and robots. So far he has failed to titillate anyone's fancy with that one, and members of the Cyborg Liberation Front follow him around the country jeering at his every word.)

As might have been expected, a few hucksters have entered the antiaging sweepstakes, offering the public everything from antigravity chambers in their basements (which are scientifically unfeasible; the whole concept is a rip-off) to Swiss Chalets on the moon (supposedly to be built within the next eighteen months; I'll believe it when I see it). The theory behind all this is that low-gravity and especially zero-gravity environments are less wearing on the body, and therefore more conducive to a long healthy lifespan. Fly-by-night home improvement operators and land development salesmen have been preying on gullibility and ignorance, as quacks have done since the beginning of time. Our fraud laws will take care of them in due course, however.

But these constitute a fringe minority, a seemingly inevitable adjunct to any new industry. The most important thing is that the legitimate technology is working. Our major diseases have been eliminated and the remaining one—aging—is now following the others into oblivion.

XII

The Paine and Jefferson of Oceana

1

The Disney organization was the first to build a self-contained community in the ocean, and other developers are planning to follow this lead during the next few years. It was virtually inevitable that Disney Enterprises would be the pioneer in the field since the company's founder, Walt Disney, had launched a revolution in community technology back in the early 1950s. First with the creation of Disneyland in California, followed by the twenty-seven-thousand-acre Walt Disney World in central Florida, WED Enterprises, Inc., entered the city planning business on a greater scale than any other company in the country. Originally denounced as a merchant of shlock, as a panderer to the most superficial tastes of the American public, Disney was later hailed as one of the great visionaries of the twentieth century by architects and city planners across the globe. In the spring of 1972 the highly respected architect, Peter Blake, visited Walt Disney World and declared it to be, "in a great many respects, the most interesting New Town in the United States. . . ."

Blake was not alone in his assessment. In the early 1970s, city planners were making pilgrimages to Disney's Florida site to discover why things were operating so smoothly there while the great cities of Europe and America were falling apart. New York City developer Mel Kaufman was so impressed by his "truly great learning experience" that he later brought his entire staff down on a field trip. Somehow, the stage-set architecture of the Disney enclave seemed to work. The atmosphere was escapist, futuristic, warm, and nostalgic at the same time, whereas Disney's critics had formerly claimed that his "comic-strip environment" would offend the sensibilities of most observers. Walt Disney had created a fantasy world which was more natural and down-to-earth than so-called realistic and functional architecture. The genius of Disney, the magic he conjured, lay in the fact that he blended the past and future in one dynamic concept. The best of the past and the most exhilarating promises of tomorrow coexisted in a single integrated unit. Escapism and realism, past and future, fantasy and naturalism—apparent contradictions in form and concept—flowed together and stimulated the imagination. His communities were dynamic. The senses registered continual excitement rather than familiarity. "Disney World is nearer to what people really want than anything architects have ever given them," said architect Robert Venturi. He was correct, if the long lines of people seeking admission were any indication.

Aside from the visual effects, Disney's technological achievements were straight out of the twenty-first century. Separate levels for services and goods and another for people existed throughout the entire complex. While Con Edison tore up the streets of New York City to fix broken lines, creating mammoth traffic jams and compounding the problems of frustrated motorists, Disney's water, electric, and sewage lines were all exposed in underground corridors for quick, unobtrusive repair. Supply tractors delivered goods along underground roadways without disturbing community life above. In our cities garbage trucks were clogging narrow arteries, offending sight, smell, and hearing, but in Disney World garbage was sucked through underground vacuum tubes to compacting sites outside the gates. While New Yorkers and other urban dwellers sweltered in slow, dirty, noisy, graffiti-covered subway cars, WED Enterprises had installed a quiet and efficient monorail system to transport people from one corner of the community to another. In addition, trains, tramcars, and minibuses ran when they were supposed to; the streets and sidewalks were free of debris; an on-site generating plant made Disney World independent of the utility companies; a private fire department operated effectively; an electronic monitoring system kept tabs on all equipment; pollution was nonexistent since all waste materials were recycled back into production; shops, schools, and condominiums built in the mid-1970s made Walt Disney World a self-contained residential/vacation community; in effect, WED Enterprises had established the world's first private government which, by all indications, was functioning far more smoothly than those we had grown accustomed to over the centuries.

Another aspect to the magic of the Disney vision, much appreciated by visitors and residents alike, was the idea of improving on reality and nature. Castles were built without time-encrusted walls and floors, complete with air conditioning and other modern conveniences. Man-made jungles provided a dangerfree environment where one could camp out in the wilds without fear of being mauled by wild animals. Disney proved beyond any shadow of doubt that nature and technology could coexist in harmony, and that technology could actually create a natural setting superior to the one we inherited as citizens of planet earth. In the middle of the last decade WED Enterprises (along with dozens of other land developers) purchased large tracts of land throughout the United States for the purpose of constructing fully-contained residential communities. The race was on. Before the decade was over, private communities were luring the citizenry away from the cities, towns, and villages of their birth. A string of these developments criss-crossed the nation, some of them futuristic, others more traditional in design. City planning—indeed the very tone and texture of daily existence—was coming more and more under the aegis of private enterprise.

2

The idea of private communities offering an escape from the confusion of urban existence probably originated (in modern times) with Fred French, the creator of Tudor City. His five-acre enclave of apartments, hotels, garages, gardens, and parks was New York City's first self-contained community-within-the-city. When the development opened in 1927, Tudor City was literally deluged with applications. The concept was an immediate success. It was the first viable alternative to suburban life. Here one could enjoy the privacy, the greenery, the safety, security, and the relaxed lifestyle of suburbia in the middle of Manhattan. Work, for most new residents, was a five-minute walk or bus ride away. The private-retreat-within-the-city was an idea whose time had come. Stuyvesant Town in lower Manhattan, Parkchester in the Bronx, and Lefrak City in Queens were erected with equal success. The public could not move in fast enough.

Vertical escape in the form of skyscrapers also caught on during this period. The first legitimate skyscraper (a structure supported by a metal skeleton rather than walls) was erected in Chicago in 1885 by the Home Insurance Company. The building evoked a cacophony of criticism from editorialists, social planners, and politicians alike. There was much pressure to outlaw high-rise buildings before they did any damage. The buildings would fall. The metal skeleton would cave in. The air in tall buildings could not circulate properly. The upper floors would become breeding grounds of malaria. Yet the race to build higher and higher buildings continued, with developers in New York and Chicago seeking to break each others' records every day. An article in the November 1896 issue of *North American Review* claimed emphatically that while "buildings of fifty or sixty stories are evidently feasible," such enormous heights will never be attempted. The higher the buildings went, the more the editorialists and politicians condemned them as "public menaces." Fortunately, the real estate industry of the day was strong enough to withstand this kind of Neanderthal, reactionary political pressure. By 1903, plans for ninety-three skyscrapers had been filed with the City of New York. While the politicians howled, the public seemed to want newer and taller buildings. Everyone enjoys a good contest, and the competition among builders was one of the best shows in town. The buildings did not collapse, windstorms did not blow them over, the much-publicized malaria epidemic failed to materialize. In 1908 the Singer Building reached the astronomical height of forty-seven stories. Five years later the Woolworth Building went up and held the record of sixty stories from 1913 until 1930—when it was deposed by the towering rocket-ship design of the Empire State Building.

The culmination of the Skyscraper Sweepstakes occurred in 1949 when a San Francisco architect named A. McSweeney submitted a proposal for a four-hundred-and-forty story building which would reach a height of one mile. The structure would be large enough to house half the population of San Francisco. It would contain a thousand stores, fifty schools, fifty movie houses, fifty nightclubs, twenty churches, ten hospitals, ten gymnasiums, and ten thousand business offices. In effect, McSweeney's building would have been the first vertical-city-within-a-city in human history. But by this time the public had lost its taste for the competition. A war had just been fought and won. Skyscrapers, like Lindbergh's solo flight across the Atlantic two decades earlier, were already becoming passé. McSweeney's project died for lack of enthusiasm.

Until the 1930s, skyscrapers were built primarily as commercial structures. One went to work in them. They were built by large corporations for the purpose of employing people in a central location. No one thought of actually living in them until the idea of the private urban enclave took hold. If Tudor City, Stuyvesant Town, Parkchester, and other *horizontal* communities were such an immediate success, why not vertical communities which could house more people on smaller patches of real estate? Land and building speculators were quick to see the handwriting on the wall. A supply-and-demand situation was taking form. Private kingdoms within the urban sprawl had already become a reality. The next logical step was to move people upward, above the clutter and the noise, where they could gaze down upon their fellow humans from their little fiefdoms in the sky. The marriage between skyscraper technology and the concept of private self-contained communities was a natural. It was one which would revolutionize the skyline of our great American cities during the middle third of the twentieth century.

3

Even while all this was taking place, a new factor entered the equation to complicate things further. Highways and rapid mass transportation allowed people to live farther away from their jobs than in the past. The exodus toward the suburbs accelerated considerably during the 1930s and especially in the years following World War II. As the middle class moved farther away from urban centers, corporations moved along with them into suburban industrial parks, which triggered a new expansion beyond suburbia into exurbia. The housing shortage in outlying areas reached a critical stage during the late 1940s. An economic vacuum was created, and an innovative land developer named William Levitt was only too eager to fill it.

Row upon row of two-bedroom houses, marketed under the title "The Little Levitt House," went up on Long Island within commuting distance of New York City and job areas in the nearby suburbs. To many architects and social commentators, Levittown was an eyesore—the first major instance of what would later be described as visual pollution. But, the simple fact was, housing communities where people could buy a home for less than eight thousand dollars were an absolute necessity. One sacrificed aesthetics for mass-produced economy housing. Before World War II, 85 percent of the builders in the United States put up one or two homes a year. Levitt came along and built four thousand homes on one site in a single year. The demand for his product was staggering. By 1951, Levittown grew to seventeen thousand four hundred and forty-two houses sheltering seventy-five thousand people (a figure which it took Stamford, Connecticut, thirty years to reach). A new variation on suburban living had taken root: the private enclave for the lower-middle class outside the city within commuting distance to work. Suburbia had traditionally been a haven for the upper-middle class; in the space of a few short years, Levitt had made it possible for lower-middle class working people to enjoy the privacy and security of the private housing development.

In 1952 Levittown II went up in Bucks County, Pennsylvania—a suburban retreat of seventeen thousand homes ranging from ten to eighteen thousand dollars. Blacks were originally excluded, then finally admitted in 1957 after a series of ugly demonstrations by screaming rock-throwing whites. Levittown III, started in 1958 in the suburbs between Camden and Trenton, New Jersey, triggered rumors that Levitt would soon be "taking over the country." In Levittown III, Levitt expanded his concept from a mere "housing development" to a fully self-contained community, including pools, parks, playgrounds, and schools. The addition of nearby shopping centers completed the picture; one only had to leave the fiefdom now to earn a living. These ugly barrack-like communities of identical houses were the prototype of the more exotic futuristic private governments of the 1980s. In some sense, William Levitt and Walt Disney might be considered the Paine and Jefferson of Oceana I and all the other private cities which will soon be sprouting in the oceans of the world. These are the men who gave the revolution in community technology its shape and substance. These are the forefathers of the new age of privately-run societies. Levitt and Disney were both accused of trying to "take over the country" in their time. The critics, as it turned out, were far too shortsighted. Both these gentlemen had more than the United States in their sights. Their individual visions, similar yet different in so many ways, are now altering the face of the entire globe.

4

The criticism of land developers in the early 1970s was on a par with that of the skyscraper builders in the late nineteenth and early twentieth centuries. There was some justification for it since the industry attracted the usual fringe element of frauds and petty racketeers. Hearings conducted by the federal government in 1972 revealed that most of the country's ten thousand developers were honest, but a substantial fraction was guilty of criminal abuses. "Many developers," said John McDowell, deputy administrator of the Office of Interstate Land Sales Registration, "never had any intention of providing the streets and other amenities they promised. . . ." Land was sold on the basis that schools, streets, sewage and water lines, parks, tennis courts, swimming pools, and other facilities would be constructed in due course, and buyers later discovered that all they owned (and would ever own) was a patch of sand in an undeveloped desert miles away from anything remotely resembling water. A site in Arizona, described in a brochure as "a booming city of the future," still remains a wasteland devoid of all the amenities usually associated with civilization. Most of these abuses were in direct violation of our fraud laws, and guilty corporations were either forced out of the land sales business altogether or else made to change their tactics.

Part of the blame rested with the public whose growing appetite for second homes (weekend retreats) and investments in real estate distorted basic common sense. By midsummer of 1972, four million Americans owned vacation homes and this number was increasing at a rate of two hundred thousand a year. *U.S. News and World Report*, *Time*, *Newsweek*, the *New Republic*, and other periodicals ran a series of articles on the "New American Land Boom," attributing the victimization of some buyers to their own gullibility. Writer Jerome Eden, in an article entitled "Land Fever . . . A National Epidemic," expressed amazement over how many investors were willing to pay sky-high prices for property they had never seen. An estimated one out of every ten houses built in 1972 was a second home, and the trend was only beginning to accelerate.

What lay behind it all?

Social critics and students of mass psychology outdid one another in the search for exotic, subterranean (if not sinister) motives. Our complex modern society had forced people to reexamine their goals in a quest for simplicity. People were turning back to nature in revulsion against capitalist materialism. In the age of technology the citizenry had to rediscover spiritual values. The public needed to hive off to a weekend retreat to explore "inner space" now that we had unlocked some of the mysteries of "outer space." The land boom reflected a desire to "go back to yesterday." The private retreat phenomenon was just one more aspect of America's "laissez faire ethos" with its accent on aggressiveness, acquisition, and the mania for new frontiers to conquer. Vance Packard, who defended the land craze as a search for stability, was attacked by Peter Michelson in the *New Republic* for his "Currier and Ives morality," and his reactionary "visits-to-grandma," "attic-mementos nostalgia." America was aggressive, destructive, materialistic, warlike, imperialistic, hopelessly sick—and land fever was just one more proof added to the formula. Americans had turned back to the domestic arena, to its unspoiled natural beauty, to satisfy their obsession for new colonies. All in all, the critics had quite a time analyzing, regurgitating, and agonizing over the latest epidemic of native American rapacity.

Realistically, the land development industry was nothing more or less than a natural outgrowth of increasing affluence and leisure. Now that Americans (and a good many Europeans) had obliterated poverty and hunger, for the most part, they raised the level of their aspirations accordingly. The old law of rising expectations was at work again. The battles for decent housing and enough food on the table had been won by the middle class, which comprised some 75 percent of the population. The struggle for survival became one for luxury and pleasure. Far from wanting to stop the clock and return to nature, the middle class was more concerned about hanging on to the *best of the past* while speeding the transition into the future. Hence: air-conditioned castles and danger-free jungles; nostalgic Swiss Chalets with the latest in furnishings and mechanical servants; campsites complete with electrical hook-ups and deodorized chemical toilets. One could relive the "good old days" without having to bear up under the filth and squalor that afflicted our grandparents; one could return to the past in safety, thanks to the technology of the present and future—not *return* to the past really, but rather *revisit* the past through the magic of the future. And Walt Disney was the man who made this dream come true for millions of Americans. He rendered their greatest fantasies into reality, and in doing so he launched a revolution in community design and planning which is only beginning to be fully understood now as we enter the middle-1980s. This was the genius and vision of Disney, and, to a lesser extent, Levitt and the large-scale land developers who followed in the 1970s. But it was Walt Disney who towered above them all, the man who (in this particular field at least) was fifty years or more ahead of his own time.

5

And so we return to the point where we started this section, after our brief tour through the near and not-so-distant past. The rush toward private, self-contained societies has moved beyond the land and onto the oceans. The land boom has evolved into a boom for *man-made environments*—on land and above it, on the oceans and eventually beneath them. A Paolo Soleri arcopolis—an entire community including industry, homes, learning centers, shops, roof gardens, plazas, theaters, fusion energy plants, manmade beaches, levitrains, monorails, people movers, Zisch boats, and skywalks for pedestrians—is already going up in the Pacific Ocean a hundred miles southwest of Los Angeles. General Electric is building a solar city in the Caribbean with controlled-environment farms and cloning stations for food production. Israeli architect Moshe Safdie recently submitted plans for a mile-high honeycomb of movable dwelling units, all arranged in a geometrical design to provide maximum privacy and space. Everywhere one turns there is evidence of a mass exodus into the new private communities. They *look* better than the old towns and cities. They *work* better and are more interesting to live in. If the trend continues, there won't be too many people left in the public sector for politicians to tax any longer.

Options. Novelty. Contrast. Competition in quality and design. Variation. Mobility. Simultaneous change and stability. These are the elements that attract the multitudes to the new communities. As recently as six or seven years ago, housing was standardized to a great extent. Building codes, zoning restrictions, and pressure from the construction industry all served to make housing expensive and conformist. Here and there the concepts of a few innovators stood out. Architects and daring professionals would buy a plot of earth somewhere off in the wilderness, beyond the narrow restraints of bureaucratic town officials, and erect structures that resembled houses of blocks, sheets of glass, poised rockets, and animated domes more than they did traditional houses. But in the cities, villages, and towns one passed row after row of family dwellings identical, or nearly identical in form and concept. Except for the more luxurious models, they were usually unexciting to look at. There was no room for creativity and innovation. Originality was prohibited by law.

The land developers came along and permitted a free market in ideas and technology to flourish. The net result has been a proliferation of challenging new options. You can move into the mile-high geometrical beehive of a Safdie or Soleri community, the domed lunarscape of a Buckminister Fuller-inspired society, the naturalistic environs of a Bernard Maybeck community where the homes are contoured to the land and seem to grow out of the hills and rocks, the stretch-fabric cities of Japan which are erected in a week, the steel-mesh and aluminum-fiber dwellings of the newest Levittowns which have long since gone multinational, reproduced towns with Colonials, Cape Cods, and Split Ranches for those who prefer the older designs in more comfortable surroundings, or any one of dozens of equally daring societies which literally stagger the senses. The new societies represent growth and change (and a corresponding sense of stability because of the vacuum they have filled), while the old towns and cities have taken on the aspects of museums—they are fun to visit and places where one can gaze upon the discarded relics of our past.

What else can one say about the new private communities? They provide the best of both worlds in the sense of urban conveniences in pollution-free natural settings. They have retained the best out of the past and made it more pleasurable through the miracle of technology. Unemployment is virtually nonexistent because there is no tax on industry and many corporations have been lured away by the attractive economic climate. Nor are there any taxes on individuals since the communities are profit-making, and obtain revenues from land sales and rentals. They are growing more and more food and produce a good percentage of the world's energy needs—also profit-making endeavors. There is no censorship of ideas and all subsidization is arranged very successfully on a voluntary basis. War is unthinkable since the new societies thrive on trade and industry rather than conquest. Criminals are required to work off the damage they have done, an innovation which has acted as a great deterrent to crime and kept the rate extremely low. Toleration is high for differing races and opinions, so long as no one attempts to impose his will on others by force. There are problems, to be sure, and the world the developers are creating is far from utopian (fortunately). An element of shlock has seeped into some communities, and there have been instances of fraud here and there. But at least there are more options than there were a decade ago. There is more contrast and diversity from one community to another. Architectural tastes and cultural levels vary drastically. Freedom of association is possible, and you can find a lifestyle of your choice.

Options. Choice. Free will. And that, B. F. Skinner notwithstanding, is what makes life so worthwhile.

6

The oceans today, the seabeds tomorrow. And the planets. This is the direction we are heading in. In thirty years modular cities will be sunk down into the oceans and human beings will move in. The technology is almost perfected, though terribly expensive now. It is a question of time before refinements and mass production make subocean communities economically sound. The exploration of outer space was taken up by private firms, following a lull in the federal space program in the middle and late 1970s. Money was raised by selling closed-circuit television tickets for exciting new events, the same way heavyweight bouts and daredevil acts a la Evel Knievel had been bringing in cartloads of lucre for decades past. The public will pay exorbitant prices for the chance to be titillated in ever more dazzling fashions.

A beer-drinking contest between the presidents of Chile and Argentina settled a border dispute and kept those two countries from going to war, and it raised half a billion dollars in net receipts which greatly benefited their sluggish economies. Other political rulers, quick to grasp the economic subtleties of this new situation, turned to televised boxing matches, track meets, arm-wrestling contests, and other novel competitions as a means of resolving disagreements. The public was spared the agony of armed conflicts erupting in various quarters of the world, and hostile nations were able to turn their antagonisms into profitmaking entertainments. The heads of myriad states—North and South Korea, Mainland China and Taiwan, Israel and Syria, Haiti and the Dominican Republic, many others—pummeled one another in public squares and drank each other under the table, and the citizenry of planet earth simply could not get enough of it. On the domestic scene, scalpers charged upwards of a hundred dollars a head to watch Hubert Humphrey and Scoop Jackson play strip poker until the wee hours of the morning for the Democratic presidential nomination in 1980—with the proceeds going toward the campaign fund.

By the early part of this year, dozens of airline companies and land developers were racing to the moon in a search for prime lunar territory. The first fully developed community will not be completed until 1990 at the earliest, yet the homesteading of Mars and points beyond is already being discussed in knowledgeable circles. The first moonwalk, achieved by the United States only fifteen years ago, already seems antiquated by today's standards (indeed, subsequent moonwalks were considered outdated and were largely ignored by the public only two years later). The original rockets and landing modules are now the Model-T Fords of space technology. Private space developers are forced by severe economic factors—namely, public apathy and the need to conjure ever more dazzling spectaculars if they are to compete successfully for private dollars—to keep advancing the level of space technology at an accelerating pace. The less imaginative have already fallen by the wayside, while the more daring and resourceful prosper continuously. The overall result has been a revitalized market in space travel and the development of the solar system now that the field is competitive.

It is virtually impossible to see where it will all lead. Vacation homes on Neptune by 2020? Excursion trips to Pluto by 2025? The possibilities are endless. Would that Walt Disney were alive today (will someone thaw him out, please, if he was really frozen at his death) to see the incredible new world he launched a little more than thirty years ago.

XIII

The New Enlightenment

1

And so we end this opus (dare one say *magnus* opus? I grow more self-indulgent by the day) where we began: on an optimistic note. 1984. The year and the novel. The novel has been with us for quite some time; the fateful year has finally arrived. George Orwell was wrong. He turned out to be a gifted novelist with a poor sense of the future.

Then again, perhaps I am being unfair to him. It may be he was merely trying to warn us against our own worst tendencies rather than create a vision of a world he thought would actually come to pass. Certainly, if he were with us today, he would be among the first to breathe a sigh of relief. I reread *1984* from time to time, and it still holds up as a fully accomplished work of art. The sheer power of its terrifying imagery remains, curdling the blood a little more with each turn of the page. The world today is quite the opposite of that portrayed in the novel, yet it is well we never completely lose sight of the Orwellian warning—of the society we might have created. It is well we blow the dust off *1984* every few years or so, and dip into its gripping pages for a look at the human condition at its worst.

Of the doomsday criers who followed Orwell—Ehrlich, the Paddocks, Luther Evans, B. F. Skinner, and others mentioned in great detail earlier in this book—I am far less tolerant. I distrust their motives, as I always have, while I do not feel that way about George Orwell. His pessimism was honest, and rooted in a genuine fear of the totalitarian tendency existing in too many of our fellow human beings. The pessimism of the Doomsday Brigade was (and remains on a smaller scale) a different matter entirely. This pessimism was based on a fear of individual liberty, and a distrust of human decency and common sense. It was pessimism whose basic thrust was toward the kind of society Orwell warned us about in his novel. It was, in fact, the Doomsday Brigade whom Orwell feared the most—this sizeable claque of gloomy, dictatorial, unimaginative men and women which constituted the ranks of the "totalitarian liberals" Orwell was so fond of attacking. This is the basic distinction between the nightmare world portrayed in *1984*, and that conjured by the Doomsday Brigade. We owe a debt to Orwell for holding up a mirror to the dark side of human nature. The Doomsday Brigade—and its political counterpart: the collectivizers of the individual man and woman—deserve nothing but unbridled contempt.

2

Throughout the long course of human history a struggle has been waged in various countries of the world. The struggle took on different aspects according to the political climate of each particular country in each particular century; but, no matter how much the events on the surface seemed to vary, the essentials were pretty much the same. These essentials were set down by Plato and Aristotle twenty-three hundred years ago, and most socio-economic-political disputes that have erupted during the intervening years followed from them.

Plato gave the world a utopian vision of a society managed by an elite group of rulers or guardians which maintained complete control over the productive classes. The "best stock" of both sexes were brought together as frequently as possible for breeding purposes, and the offspring carted off to "rearing pens" to be raised by professional nurses working for the state. All property was held in common, and goods and pleasures were shared communally; privacy in both the material and spiritual life of the citizenry was forbidden. Each individual was assigned a trade best suited to him or her by nature. Plato's Republic was static, rigid, and totalitarian. It was ruled by gifted guardians who renounced property and other material goods, married and procreated for the state, and scorned individuality in all their affairs. Aristotle's view of humanity and society was altogether different. He maintained that everyone possessed the capacity to know and understand the objective world through the power of reason. For Aristotle there was no special elite, no select group which was ordained by nature to preside over the affairs of the rest of humanity. Aristotle believed in the individual as the basic unit of society, the family as its cornerstone, and the autonomy of individual thought and reason in determining the course of human events. Plato's utopian paradise was elitist and dictatorial; Aristotle's society individualistic and logical. The tug-of-war that has erupted in various nations over the centuries is rooted in the Platonic/Aristotelian dichotomy (gray areas exist, of course, but in broad terms the dichotomy holds up). By and large, our long historical struggles have been between those who seek to control others through political and military force on one hand, and, on the other, those who believe that human liberty is a natural right and people should be left alone to regulate their own affairs.

The Platonic heritage has been a long time dying. We saw it emerge again in Thomas More's oppressive *Utopia,* where all homes were uniform in size and architecture, the people were obliged to put in two years of agricultural service for the state regardless of their trade, the hours for sleep, eating, and labor were strictly regulated, slavery was institutionalized, and no travel was permitted without the consent of the authorities. As if this vision of paradise on earth were not enough to satisfy the power lust of would-be dictators throughout Europe, another gentleman named Tommaso Campanella came trotting down the pike a century later with a scenario straight out of the flaming depths of hell. His Utopia would be built on a hill and governed by a consecrated Prince called Metaphysic. Metaphysic was to be assisted by three lesser Princes: Power, Knowledge, and Love. Private property would be (surprise!) abolished, and the hour of coupling would be fixed by astrologers to guarantee a healthy race (totalitarians through the ages, whether of the Right or of the Left, have all been inordinately concerned about the *quality* of the species). Coitus for pleasure was to be permitted with pregnant and sterile women only, and sodomists would be required to wear a shoe around their necks to show the world they have put "their feet where the head should have been."

After Campanella, it appeared virtually impossible that anyone would outdo his Platonic paradise in both phantasmagoric imagery and passion—but that did not stop others from trying. Valentin Andrae declared in 1619 that man was inherently wicked, and he called for weekly investigations into public morality to banish cursing, gambling, luxuriousness, quarreling, conceit, and a host of other heinous sins. His ideal society would be ruled by a triumvirate which would hold all goods and property in common, and apportion them equally among the populace. Francis Bacon's *New Atlantis* was run along scientific lines with a ruling elite of scientists who owned all knowledge and used it for the "common good." Thomas Hobbes advocated an absolute monarchy in his *Leviathan,* published in 1651; Gabriel de Foigny wanted his Utopia presided over by an Old Man Philosopher; in the nineteenth century Marx and Engels crystallized Platonic collectivism into a more modern version of industrialized socialism; and these fathers of contemporary socialism gave birth to later generations of progressives, Bolsheviks, fascists, Nazis, psychological behaviorists, Maoists, Castroites, totalitarian liberals, and doomsday alarmists, all of whom subscribed to the same basic premises: private property is evil, free trade is immoral, the individual is a mere cog in a giant machine called mass society, and only an elite group of social planners knows what's best for the giant machine and can save it from self-destruction.

3

Notable voices have been raised in condemnation of the Platonic inheritance over the centuries. Great satirists like Aristophanes, Rabelais, Swift, and Voltaire, and curmudgeons like Twain, Mencken, and Waugh have skewered the collectivist mentality with their pens and held it up for public ridicule. More serious writers like Aquinas, James Harrington, Spencer, Locke, Paine, Jefferson, and Thoreau concerned themselves with the philosophical questions regarding the relationship between the individual and his fellow human beings. In broad general terms they defended the rights of the individual against the arbitrary rule of a power elite bent on total control.

Despite this formidable opposition, the Platonists have managed to reign supreme in the political arena throughout most of human history. The emperors, kings, czars, and one-party dictators of modern times have dominated the great multitudes of the earth and, with the help of intellectuals and writers tutored in the collectivist mold, have convinced the overwhelming majority of peoples of the legitimacy of their authoritarian rule. The Divine Right of Dictatorship was most successfully challenged in 1776 by a committed band of Aristotelians who declared their independence from an English king. Paine. Jefferson. Henry. Sam Adams. The Age of Reason. Common Sense. The Rights of Man. Life. Liberty. The Right to own property and pursue happiness. An intellectual ferment, the likes of which the earth had never before witnessed, all came to a head in the American revolution. A ferment of passion and ideas. A maelstrom of events centered on the individual and his fundamental rights as a citizen of planet earth.

Thomas Paine kicked it all off with his pamphlet *Comman Sense*, but it was Jefferson who symbolized the great new renaissance in human thought. He, above all others, carried the Aristotelian premise further along the way to its final social and philosophical conclusions. Life, liberty, and happiness were not gifts to be dispensed among the multitudes by a fickle ruler; they were natural rights possessed absolutely by the people. By improving on Harrington, Winstanley, and Locke who came before him, Jefferson set the tone for the revolution with his Declaration of Independence—a document into which he poured the full power of his intellectual passions. The hunger for individual liberty would soon alter the course of human history. In Europe, the old order was being shaken and throttled to the foundation. Its medieval walls were crumbling and letting in gusts of air—the radical winds of freedom. With each breeze the passion for freedom was inflamed anew, every gust fanning the flames into a single roiling inferno.

The dream was aborted for a while, somewhere along the way. Slavery, wars, and an insidious resurgence of Platonic collectivism all combined to derail the Aristotelian renaissance. Marxism, totalitarian liberalism, and a hybrid blend of fascism and socialism threatened to drive us backward in time, back to medieval primitivism, back to the Dark Ages, back to the long black night of the human soul.

Yet, the revolution survived. The freedoms we fought for have been reaffirmed.

Reason prevailed over irrationality; liberty over slavery; creativity over destruction; life over death. We have entered a new era now, not only in America, but throughout the entire globe. A New Age of Reason. A New Enlightenment. Nothing less than a revolution of the human spirit. World peace now seems assured. Universal freedom is all but inevitable. Free trade and association among all people and societies is the order of the day. The grim shadow of slavery has *not* fallen over the earth. There are options open to humanity. There is diversity, variety, eccentricity, spontaneity, and happiness. The dictators have not succeeded. After a long dark night in the human condition, the Aristotelian ideal has finally triumphed.

Yet, we dare not become too smug or complacent.

Those who despise man and his freedoms have not abandoned the fight entirely; they are only silent for the moment.

They await the proper time to strike again and destroy the civilization they have come to hate more and more over the past decades.

They detest the individual, his and her triumphs, genius, talents, ingenuity, originality, and creativity.

They cannot tolerate human achievement; they despise accomplishment and virtue.

They nourish themselves on fear and hatred. These emotions are the very substance of their existence.

We best remain alert with Jefferson, when he warned: "The price of liberty is eternal vigilance."

We ignore his admonition at our own risk.

1984 will soon be behind us. We damned well better make sure it never returns to haunt us again.

Bibliography

BOOKS

James Truslow Adams, *The Epic of America,* Little, Brown, and Co., 1931.

——*March of Democracy*, vol. II, Charles Scribner's Sons, 1932.

Charles Abrams, *Revolution in Land,* Harper and Brothers, 1939.

William Bailie, *Josiah Warren: The First American Anarchist,* Arno Press, reprint, 1972.

Hilaire Belloc, *The Restoration of Property,* Sheed and Ward, 1936.

Marie Louise Berneri, *Journey Through Utopia,* Books for Libraries Press, reprint, 1969.

Barbara Brown, *New Mind, New Body,* Harper and Row, 1974.

V. F. Calverton, *Where Angels Dared to Tread,* Bobbs-Merrill, 1941.

Adolfo Bioy Casares, *Diary of the War of the Pig,* McGraw-Hill, 1972.

Francis W. Coker, *Democracy, Liberty, and Property,* The Macmillan Company, 1942.
Sebastian de Grazia, *Of Time, Work, and Leisure,* The Twentieth Century Fund, 1962.
Gottfried Dietze, *In Defense of Property,* Henry Regnery Company, 1963.
Frank Friedel, ed., *The New Deal and the American People,* Prentice-Hall, 1964.
Mary Anne Guitar, *Property Power,* Doubleday and Co., 1968.
Christopher Hill, *The World Turned Upside Down: Radical Ideas During the English Revolution,* The Viking Press, 1972.
Matthew Josephson, *The Robber Barons,* Harcourt, Brace and Co., 1934.
Herman Kahn and B. Bruce-Briggs, *Things to Come: Thinking About the 70's and 80's,* The Macmillan Company, 1972.
Robert Katz, *A Giant in the Earth,* Stein and Day, 1973.
Robert Rives La Monte, Socialist, and H. L. Mencken, Individualist, *Men Versus the Man,* Arno Press, reprint, 1972.
Christopher Lasch, *The World of Nations,* Alfred A. Knopf, 1973.
William E. Leuchtenburg, *Franklin D. Roosevelt and the New Deal,* Harper and Row, 1963.
Frank E. Manuel, ed., *Utopias and Utopian Thought,* Houghton Mifflin Company, 1965.
Thomas Molnar, *Utopia: The Perennial Heresy,* Sheed and Ward, 1967.
Samuel R. Ogden, ed., *America the Vanishing,* The Stephen Greene Press, 1969.
H. A. Overstreet, *A Guide to Civilized Loafing,* W. W. Norton and Co., 1934.
Vance Packard, *A Nation of Strangers,* David McKay, 1972.
Vernon Louis Parrington, Jr., *American Dreams,* Russell and Russell, Inc., 1964.
James T. Patterson, *The New Deal and the States,* Princeton University Press, 1969.
Richard H. Pells, *Radical Visions and American Dreams,* Harper and Row, 1973.
Dennis C. Pirages and Paul R. Ehrlich, *Ark II,* The Viking Press, 1974.
Irving Price, *Buying Country Property,* Harper and Row, 1972.
Samuel Putnam, ed., *The Portable Rabelais,* The Viking Press, 1946.

Eugene Rachlis and John E. Marqusee, *The Land Lords,* Random House, 1963.
Lawrence Rocks and Richard Runyan, *The Energy Crisis,* Crown, 1972.
O. E. Rölvaag, *Giants in the Earth,* Harper and Row, 1927.
Lydia Rosier, ill., *The Best Nature Writing of Joseph Wood Krutch,* William Morrow and Co., 1969, 1970.
Leonard R. Sayles and Margaret K. Chandler, *Managing Large Systems,* Harper and Row, 1971.
Charles T. Sprading, *Liberty and the Great Libertarians,* Arno Press, reprint, 1972.
Kurt Stehling, *Computers and You,* The World Publishing Company, 1972.
William Graham Sumner, *What Social Classes Owe to Each Other,* Arno Press, reprint, 1972.
Jerome Tuccille, *Here Comes Immortality,* Stein and Day, 1973.
Rexford G. Tugwell, *In Search of Roosevelt,* Harvard University Press, 1972.
William van Dusen, *The Natural Depth in Man,* Harper and Row, 1972.
Various authors, *Population Control: For and Against,* Hart Publishing Company, 1973.
Thorstein Veblen, *The Theory of the Leisure Class,* Houghton Mifflin, reprint, 1973.
William H. Whyte, *The Last Landscape,* Doubleday and Co., 1968.

ARTICLES AND OTHER REFERENCES

"The World of Buckminster Fuller" (*Architectural Forum,* Jan.-February 1972).
"The Worst Is Yet to Be?" (*Time,* January 24, 1972).
"Paolo Soleri: Urban Prophet in the Arizona Desert," By Robert B. Kaiser (*Saturday Review,* February 12, 1972).
"New American Land Rush" (*Time,* February 28, 1972).
"Yes, Amateurs Do Make Money in Real Estate" (*Changing Times,* March 1972).
"Rural Land Is Going! Going! Gone!" by Carole G. Rogers (*McCall's, April 1972).*

"3-Day Week Stirs Dispute in Jersey," by Fred Ferretti (New York Times, April 6, 1972).
"In Pursuit of the Second Home" (*Newsweek,* April 17, 1972).
"My New Hexa-Pent Dome: Designed for You to Live In," by R. Buckminster Fuller (*Popular Science,* May 1972).
"Florida's Master Real Estate Sleuth" (*Business Week,* May 20, 1972).
"Land Fever . . . A National Epidemic," by Jerome Eden (*Field and Stream,* July 1972).
"The Recreational Land Rip-Off," by Paul M. Sears (*New Republic,* July 8, 1972).
"Sheltering the Senses," by Ronald Najman *(Saturday Review,* August 12, 1972).
"Vacation Homes—A Boom with Pitfalls" (*U.S. News and World Report,* August 14, 1972).
"Fitting a House to the Land," by Leslie Mandelson Freudenheim and Elisabeth Sussman (*Saturday Review,* Sept. 9, 1972).
"Mobile Homes: The New Ghettos," by Frank Trippett (*Saturday Review,* Sept. 23. 1972).
"A New Power on the Campus" (*Think,* October 1972).
"A Tranquil Canadian Island Resists the U.S. Speculator," by William Borders (*New York Times,* Oct. 2, 1972).
"Where Did Neighborhoods Go?" by Peter Michelson (*New Republic,* Oct. 7, 1972).
"Builder Presses Mixed Unit Plan" (*New York Times,* Oct. 8, 1972).
"11 Floors May Be Added to the Empire State," by Deidre Carmody (*New York Times,* Oct. 11, 1972).
"Flood Perils Grow as Land Is Covered by Developer," by Seth S. King (*New York Times,* Oct. 14, 1972).
"The Developers Are Coming," by J. Anthony Lukas (*Saturday Review,* Oct. 21, 1972).
"Mickey Mouse Teaches the Architects," by Paul Goldberger (*New York Times Magazine,* Oct. 22, 1972).
"Housing Study: High Rise = High Crime," by Jack Rosenthal (*New York Times,* Oct. 26, 1972).
"Civic Groups Are Investigating Canarsie Blockbusting Reports," by Paul L. Montgomery (*New York Times,* Nov. 3, 1972).

"Building Geodesic Dome Tests Skills of Students" (*New York Times,* Nov. 4, 1972).
"Housing Complex Planned for 42,000 in Manhattan," by Robert D. McFadden (*New York Times,* Nov. 5, 1972).
"Innovators Elbow Traditions Aside," by William G. Connolly (*New York Times,* Nov. 5, 1972).
"Land Fraud Target of U.S. Crackdown," by Donald Janson (*New York Times,* Nov. 26, 1972).
Entire issue (*Reason*, December 1972).
"Air Structures: Inflatable Alternatives," by Joseph M. Valerio (*Saturday Review*, Dec. 23, 1972).
"America: Inventing a Nation," by Alistaire Cooke (NBC-TV, Dec. 26, 1972).
"Butter-Pecan Builder" (*Time,* Jan. 8, 1973).
Entire issue (*Canada Today,* February 1973).
"The Free Flow of Technology," by Richard Bode (*Think,* March 1973).
"Disputed Drug Is Restudied for Use in Geriatrics," by Harold M. Schmeck, Jr. (*New York Times,* March 18, 1973).
"The Green Revolution Hasn't Ended Hunger," by James P. Sterba (*New York Times,* April 15, 1973).
"Can Aging Be Cured?" (*Time,* April 16, 1973).
"A Cleaner Hudson Keeps Shad Fisherman Busy," by Nelson Bryant (*New York Times,* April 28, 1973).
"Learning to Love New Again," by David M. Rorvik (*Esquire,* May 1973).
"The Energy Crisis: Time for Action" (*Time,* May 7, 1973).
"More About Herpes" (*Time,* May 7, 1973).
"Near a Nuclear Plant, Outdoor Laboratory Keeps Tabs on Environment," by John Noble Wilford (*New York Times,* May 11, 1973).
"Revolution Near at Check-Out Counter," by John D. Morris (*New York Times,* May 21, 1973).
"English Cow Gives Birth to Calf Grown from 2d Cow's Embryo" (*New York Times,* June 8, 1973).
"Doctors Study Treating of Ills Brought on by Stress," by Jane E. Brody (*New York Times,* June 10, 1973).
"'Second Home' Craze is Threatening Serenity of Big Alpine Region," by Paul Hofmann (*New York Times,* June 16, 1973).
"Chicago 21" (*Time,* July 2, 1973).

"Roughing It the Easy Way" (*Time,* July 2, 1973).

"The Multinational Corporation Tightrope," by Walter E. Schirmer (speech delivered July 6, 1973).

"Copionics Bulletin" (World Economic Organization, September 1973).

"Data Banks to the Rescue," by Richard Bode (*Think,* September 1973).

"Bigger Role for Computer in U.S. Health Care," by Richard Bode (*Think,* October 1973).

"On the History of Our Energy Gap," by Frank N. Ikard (letter to the *New York Times,* Feb. 28, 1974).

Entire issue (*World Citizen Federalist Letter,* March 1974).

Entire issue (*World Citizen Federalist Letter,* April 1974).

"As Birth Rate Drops, So Does Interest in It," by Douglas E. Kneeland (*New York Times,* April 4, 1974).

"Arnold Toynbee: Are Businessmen Creating a New Pax Romana?" interview conducted by James Flanagan (*Forbes,* April 15, 1974).

"Famine Specter Haunts UN Delegates," by Associated Press (*Reporter Dispatch,* April 25, 1974).

"End of Smallpox in 1975 Predicted" (*New York Times,* May 1, 1974).

"It Was 1949, And Here's How Some Saw the Future," by Robert D. McFadden (*New York Times,* May 1, 1974).

"Declines in Deaths from Nine Leading Diseases Show a Surprising Trend," by Harold M. Schmeck, Jr. (*New York Times,* May 6, 1974.)

"Political Watershed for France," by Flora Lewis (*New York Times,* May 9, 1974).

"Seizure of Property by Nasser Is Ruled Illegal by Cairo Court," by Henry Tanner (*New York Times,* May 9, 1974).

"Hydrogen—A Way Out of the Energy Crisis?" by Victor K. McElheny (*New York Times,* May 12, 1974).

"Nuclear Fusion Reported in Lab with Aid of Laser," by Harold M. Schmeck, Jr. (*New York Times,* May 14, 1974).

"'People's Van' Travels the Low-Cost Route to Coast," by Robert Lindsey (*New York Times,* May 14, 1974).

"Peril to 400 Million Is Seen by UNICEF," by Kathleen Teltsch (*New York Times,* May 14, 1974).

"Solar Challenge," by Peter E. Glaser (letter to the *New York Times,* May 20, 1974).

"The Case for Free Enterprise," by William J. Carney (letter to the *New York Times,* May 25, 1974).
"WHO Confident Smallpox Can Be Erased in Years Despite India Epidemic," by Lawrence K. Altman (*New York Times,* June 7, 1974).
"Geothermal Power Hunted in Montana," by Edward Cowan (*New York Times,* June 9, 1974).
"New City Planned in South Jersey," by Donald Janson (*New York Times,* June 17, 1974).
"1984: Here Today, Here Tomorrow?" by Nicholas von Hoffman (*Washington Post,* June 17, 1974).
"The Year 2000 in India: Experts Paint Grim Picture," by Bernard Weinraub (*New York Times,* June 19, 1974).
"The Right to Privacy," by Edward I. Koch (letter to the *New York Times,* July 4, 1974).
"Brain 'Pacemakers' Would Watch More Than Brain," by Richard M. Restak (*New York Times,* July 7, 1974).
"Heart Deaths Down," by Lawrence Feinberg (*Washington Post,* July 10, 1974).
"Energy Crisis of 1974 Fades Away, But Impact Lingers On," by Edward C. Burks (*New York Times,* July 12, 1974).
"Gain Made on Goal of Fusion Power," by Walter Sullivan (*New York Times,* July 12, 1974).
"Oil Supplies Exceed Levels of a Year Ago" (*New York Times,* July 12, 1974).
"Fears Over Food Growing in India," by Bernard Weinraub (*New York Times,* July 15, 1974).
Interview with Richard Bode (July 15, 1974).
"Human Births Reported from Eggs Fertilized in Lab" (*New York Times,* July 16, 1974).
"Smallpox Grows in India; Worst Over, Officials Say," by Bernard Weinraub (*New York Times,* July 16, 1974).
"Not by Claw Alone," by Joan Marble Cook (*New York Times,* July 25, 1974).
"Computer 'Model' of World Sought to Cope with Food Shortage," by Walter Sullivan (*New York Times,* August 10, 1974).
"Population Boom and Food Shortage: World Losing Fight for Vital Balance," by Gladwin Hill (*New York Times,* Aug. 14, 1974).

"Effort to Stop Shanker Fails in A.F.T.," by Gene I. Maeroff (*New York Times,* Aug. 21, 1974).
"Farm Experts See a U.S. Opportunity to Lessen Hunger," by William Robbins (*New York Times,* Aug. 25, 1974).
"World Agency Proposed for the Fight on Hunger," by William Robbins (*New York Times,* Aug. 28, 1974).
"New Corn Type Exceeds Beef in Quality of Protein," by Boyce Rensberger (*New York Times,* Sept. 4, 1974).
"Smile. The Prophets of Gloom and Doom Are Not All Right," by Colin Greer (*New York Times,* Sept. 4, 1974).
"Scientists Seek to Breed a 'Super Plant' to Guarantee Food Supply," by Boyce Rensberger (*New York Times,* Sept. 5, 1974).
"Disney, Expert in Mass Transit, Offers to Aid Cities," by Robert Lindsey (*New York Times,* Sept. 10, 1974).
"Gain Reported in Halting Aging in Cells," by Lawrence K. Altman (*New York Times,* Sept. 20, 1974).
"Green Revolution Passes Over Asia Without Expected Upheaval," by Victor K. McElheny (*New York Times,* Sept. 23, 1974).